The Pocket Guide to

Critical Thinking

Third Edition

Richard L. Epstein
Carolyn Kernberger

Advanced Reasoning Forum

THOMSON

™

WADSWORTH

Australia • Canada • Mexi

Spain • United King

D0322302

Publisher: *Holly J. Allen*   Illustrator: *Alex Raffi*
Philosophy Editor: *Steve Wainwright* Assistant Editor: *Lee McCracken*
Marketing Manager: *Worth Hawes*   Cover Designer: *Yvo Riezebos*
Print Media Buyer: *Lisa Claudeanos* Project Manager: *Jerry Holloway*
Permissions Editor: *Chelsea Junget*   Printer: *West Group*
Advertising Project Manager: *Laurel Anderson*

Printed in the United States of America.
1 2 3 4 5 6 7 09 08 07 06 05

Names, characters, and incidents relating to any of the characters in this text are used fictitiously, and any resemblance to actual persons, living or dead, is entirely coincidental.

For more information about our products, contact us at:
Thomson Learning Academic Resource Center at 1–800–423–0563
For permission to use material from this text, submit a request online:
http://www.thomsonrights.com
Any additional questions about permissions can be submitted to
thomsonrights@thomson.com

Thomson Higher Education **Canada**
10 Davis Drive   Thomson Nelson
Belmont, CA 94002–3098   1120 Birchmount Road
USA   Toronto, Ontario M1K 5G4, Canada

Asia   **Australia/New Zealand**
Thomson Learning   Thomson Learning Australia
5 Shenton Way   102 Dodds Street
#01–01 UIC Building   Southbank, Victoria 3006
Singapore 068808   Australia

Library of Congress Control Number: 2004110965
ISBN 0-534-58429-2

The Pocket Guide to Critical Thinking
Third Edition

Preface

This little book is meant as a summary and guide to the art of reasoning well.

Critical thinking is evaluating whether we should be convinced that some claim is true or some argument is good, as well as formulating good arguments. Critical thinking is something we need to do every day.

We've summarized here the most important ideas about the subject. But critical thinking is more than knowing definitions and rules and a few examples. It requires judgment. The full story, with lots of examples and exercises, is in our textbook *Critical Thinking*. Use this *Pocket Guide* as a place to start learning how to reason well and write good arguments, or as a summary for reference. Your practice can come from using these ideas every day studying, watching television, reading the newspaper, browsing the Web, working at your job, and talking to your friends and family.

Many sections of the text can be read independently, though Chapter 1 and Sections 1, 2, and 4 of Chapter 2 are essential for the material following that follows. The discussions of explanations and models in Chapter 5 also depend on the material in Chapter 4. In this third edition we have added sections on graphs and on prescriptive claims. As well, the discussion of models has been expanded to make clearer the relation of reasoning with models and confirming theories by experiment.

Because your reasoning can be sharpened, you can understand more, you can avoid being duped. You can reason well with those you love and work with and need to convince. But whether you will do so depends not just on method, not just on the tools of reasoning, but on your goals, your ends. And that depends on virtue.

1   Claims

We want to arrive at truths from our reasoning. So we need to be able to recognize whether a sentence is true or false—or whether it is just nonsense. And if it is true or false, does that depend on what someone thinks, or is it independent of people? What standard is being invoked? Section 1.1 is devoted to the nature of claims.

To reason well, we need to understand the words we and others use. Definitions are a good way to clarify our thinking. In Section 1.2 we study how to make and recognize good definitions.

Before we turn to the nature of arguments, we'll look at ways people try to convince us without reasoning. In Section 1.3 we look at how claims can be concealed by manipulation of language by using loaded questions and other slanters.

1.1 Claims

> *Claim* A declarative sentence used in such a way that it is either true or false (but not both).

Example 1 Dogs are mammals.
 Analysis This is a claim.

Example 2 $2 + 2 = 5$
 Analysis This is a claim, a false claim.

Example 3 Dick is hungry.
 Analysis This is a claim, even if we don't know if it's true.

Example 4 How can anyone be so dumb to think cats can reason?
 Analysis This is not a claim. Questions are not claims, even if meant to be taken rhetorically.

Example 5 I wish I could get a job.
 Analysis Whether this is a claim depends on how it's used. If Maria, who's been trying to get a job for three weeks says this to herself, it's not a claim—we don't say that a wish is true or false. But if Dick's parents are berating him for not getting a job, he might say, "It's not that I'm not trying. I wish I could get a job." Since he could be lying, in that context it is a claim.

Often what people say is *too vague* to take as a claim— there's no single obvious way to understand the words that we can take to be true or false. For example:

> You can win a lot playing blackjack.
> Our dish soap is new and improved.
> People who are disabled are just as good as people who aren't.

But everything we say is somewhat vague. After all, no two people have identical perceptions, and since the way we understand words depends on our experience, we all understand words a little differently.

Example 6   Tom: My English professor showed up late for class
on Tuesday.
   Analysis   Which Tuesday? Who's his English professor?
What does he mean by late? Five minutes? Thirty seconds?
How does he determine when she showed up? When she walked
through the door? At exactly what point? When her nose crossed
the threshold? That's silly. We all know "what he meant."

   It isn't whether a sentence is vague, but whether it's too
vague, given the context, for us to be justified in saying
it has a truth-value. It's a mistake, a *drawing the line
fallacy*, to argue that if you can't make the difference
precise, there's no difference. In an auditorium lit by a single
candle some parts are clearly lit and some parts are clearly
dark, even if we can't draw a precise line where it stops being
light and starts being dark. Often we pick out a common
mistake in reasoning and call it a *fallacy*.

Example 7   If a suspect who is totally uncooperative is hit once
by a policeman, then that's not unnecessary force. Nor twice, if
he's resisting. Possibly three times. If he's still resisting,
shouldn't the policeman have the right to hit him again? It would
be dangerous not to allow that. So, you can't tell me exactly how
many times a policeman has to hit a suspect before it's unnecessary
force. So the policeman did not use unnecessary force.
   Analysis   This convinced the jury in the first trial of the
policemen who beat up Rodney King in L.A. in the '90s. But it's
bad reasoning, an example of the drawing the line fallacy.

   A basic divide in claims is between those that are about
the world outside our minds and those about mental states.

Subjective and objective claims   A claim is
subjective if whether it is true or false depends on
what someone (or something or some group) thinks,
believes, or feels. A subjective claim invokes
personal standards. Claims that are not subjective
are *objective* and use *impersonal standards*.

Example 8   All ravens are black.
Analysis   This is an objective claim.

Example 9   My dog is hungry.
Analysis   This is a subjective claim.

Example 10   It's cold outside.
Analysis   This is too vague to be an objective claim. But if the speaker means just that it seems cold to him, then it's a subjective claim.

Example 11   Harry: New cars today are really expensive.
Analysis   If Harry means that new cars cost too much for him to feel comfortable buying one, then the claim is subjective. If Harry has in mind that the average cost of a new car is more than twice the federal government poverty standard for a family of four, then he would be using impersonal standards, and the claim is objective. Or Harry may have no standard in mind, in which case what he's said is too vague to be taken as a claim. *If it is not clear what standard is being invoked, then the sentence is too vague to be classified as a claim.*

Example 12   Wanda weighs 215 pounds.
Analysis   This is an objective claim.

Example 13   Wanda is fat.
Analysis   This is a subjective claim, depending on what the speaker considers fat. But what if Wanda is so obese that everyone would consider her fat? It's still subjective, but since everyone would agree on that standard, we say it's *intersubjective.*

Example 14   God exists.
Analysis   Often people think that a lot of disagreement about whether a claim is true means that the claim is subjective. But that's a confusion, the *subjectivist fallacy.* Whatever we mean by "God" it's supposed to be something that exists independently of people. The example is objective.

Example 15   Zoe: That tie is hideous.
       Dick: What are you talking about? It's great, the new style.
       Zoe: You're crazy, it's ugly.
Analysis   Dick and Zoe are treating a subjective claim as objective. There's no sense in arguing about taste.

1.2 Definitions

> **Definition**   A definition is an explanation or stipulation of how to use a word or phrase.

A definition is not a claim.   A definition is not true or false, but good or bad, apt or wrong. Definitions tell us what we're talking about.

Example 1   "Exogenous" means "developing from without."
   Analysis   This is a definition, not a claim. It is an explanation of how to use the word "exogenous."

Example 2   Puce is the color of a flea, purple-brown or brownish-purple.
   Analysis   This is a definition, not a claim.

Example 3   Abortion is the murder of unborn children.
   Analysis   This is a *persuasive definition*: a claim masquerading as a definition. What should be debated is being assumed in the definition. It's bad to use persuasive definitions.

Example 4   A feminist is someone who thinks that women are better than men.
   Analysis   This is a persuasive definition.

Example 5   —Maria's so rich, she can afford to buy you dinner.
   —What do you mean by "rich"?
   —She's got a Mercedes.
   Analysis   This is not a definition—or it's a very bad one. Some people who have a Mercedes aren't rich, and some people who are rich don't own one. That Maria has a Mercedes is some *evidence* that she's rich.

Example 6   Intuition is perception via the unconscious.
                                                    Carl G. Jung

5

Analysis This is a definition, but a bad one. The words doing the defining are no clearer than what's being defined.

Example 7 Fasting and very low calorie diets (diets below 500 calories) cause a loss of nitrogen and potassium in the body, a loss which is believed to trigger a mechanism in the body that causes us to hold on to our fat stores and to turn to muscle protein for energy instead.   *Jane Fonda's New Workout and Weight Loss Program*

Analysis Definitions are not always labeled, but are often made in passing. This is a good definition of "very low calorie diet."

Good definition   For a definition to be good, both:
- The words doing the defining are clear and better understood than the word or phrase being defined.
- The words being defined and the defining phrase can be used interchangeably. That is, it's correct to use the one exactly when it's correct to use the other.

The key to making a good definition is to look for examples where the definition does or does not apply to make sure the definition is not too broad (covers cases it shouldn't) or too narrow (misses cases it should cover).

Example 8 Suppose we want to define "school cafeteria." That's something a lawmaker might need in order to write a law to disburse funds for a food program. As a first go, we might try "A place in a school where students eat." But that's too broad, since that would include a room with no food service where students can take their meals. So we could try "A place in a school where students can buy a meal." But that's also too broad, since it would include a room where students could buy a sandwich from a vending machine. How about "A room in a school where students can buy a hot meal that is served on a tray"? But if there's a fast-food restaurant like Burger King at the school, that would qualify. So it looks like we need "A room in a school where students can buy a hot meal that is served on a tray, and the school is responsible for the preparation and selling of the food." This looks better, though if adopted as a definition in a law it might keep schools that want money from the legislature from contracting out the preparation of their food. Whether the definition is too narrow will depend on how the lawmakers intend the money to be spent.

Steps in making a good definition

- Show the need for a definition.
- State the definition.
- Make sure the words make sense.
- Give examples where the definition applies.
- Give examples where the definition does not apply.
- If necessary, contrast it with other likely definitions.
- Possibly revise your definition.

1.3 Concealed Claims

> **Slanter**   A slanter is any choice of words meant to convince by concealing a dubious claim.

Slanters are bad because they try to get us to assume a dubious claim is true without reflecting on it. In this section we'll look at some common types of slanters.

Often people try to conceal a claim with a question that presupposes it is true.

> When are you planning to start studying in this course?
> Why don't you love me anymore?
> Why can't you dress like a gentleman?

The best response to a *loaded question* is to point out the concealed claim and begin discussing that.

A *euphemism* (yoo´-fuh-mizm) is a word or phrase that makes something sound better than a neutral description. In contrast, a *dysphemism* (dis´-fuh-mizm) makes something sound worse than a neutral description.

Example 1   Suzy: You should try to fix up Wanda with a date. You can tell your friends that she's Rubenesque.
> Tom: You mean she's fat.
> *Analysis* Suzy's used a euphemism.

Example 2   The freedom fighter attacked the convoy.
> *Analysis* "Freedom fighter" is a euphemism, concealing the claim that the guerillas are good people fighting to liberate their country and give their countrymen freedom.

Example 3   The terrorists attacked the convoy.
> *Analysis* "Terrorist" is a euphemism, concealing the claim that the guerillas are bad people, inflicting violence on civilians for their own partisan ends without popular support.

A *downplayer* is a word or phrase that minimizes the significance of a claim; an *up-player* exaggerates.

Example 4 Zoe: Hey Mom. Great news. I managed to pass my first French exam.

Mom: You only just passed?

Analysis Zoe has up-played the significance of what she did, concealing the claim "It took great effort to pass" with the word "managed." Her mother downplayed the significance of passing by using "only just," concealing the claim "Passing and not getting a good grade is not commendable."

One way to downplay is with *qualifiers*, words that restrict or limit the meaning of others.

Example 5 If you buy this book, you'll get a job paying 25% more than the average wage in the U.S.*

A *weaseler* is a claim that's qualified so much that the apparent meaning is no longer there.

Example 6 Maria (to her boss): I am truly sorry that it has taken so long for you to understand what I have been saying.

Analysis Maria has weaseled out of an apology.

A *proof substitute* is a way to convince by suggesting that you have a proof, but not actually offering one.

Example 7 Dr. E: By now you must have been convinced what a great teacher I am. It's obvious to anyone. Of course, some people are a little slow. But surely you see it.

Analysis Dr. E didn't prove that he's a great teacher, though he made it sound as if he were proving something. He was just reiterating the claim, trying to browbeat his students into believing it with the words "obvious," "some people are a little slow," "surely," "must have been convinced."

Another way to conceal that you have no support for your claim is to *shift the burden of proof*.

---

* Purchaser agrees to study this book four hours per day for 12 years.

Example 8   Tom: The university should lower tuition.
             Maria: Why?
             Tom: Why not?
Analysis   Tom hasn't given any reason to think his claim is
true. He's only invited Maria to say why she thinks it's false, so he
can attack that—which is easier than supporting a position.

You may be tempted to use slanters in your own writing.
Don't. Slanters turn off those you want to convince. And
though they may work for the moment, they don't stick. The
other person will remember only the joke or jibe. A good
argument can last and last. And if you use slanters, the other
person can destroy your points not by facing your arguments,
but by pointing out the slanters. If you reason calmly and
well you will earn the respect of the other, and may learn that
the other merits your respect, too.

Example 9   Wages for the same kind of labor are lower in the
South than in the North. Also, wages are lower in Puerto Rico than
in the United States. How can a northern employee protect his
wage level from the competition of lower-wage southern labor?
And how can a laborer in the United States protect his job (and
higher wage rate) from Puerto Rican labor? One device would be
to advocate "equal pay for equal work" in the United States,
including Puerto Rico, by legislating minimum wages higher than
the prevailing level in the South and Puerto Rico. It should come
as no surprise to learn that in the United States support for
minimum-wage laws comes primarily from northerners who
profess to be trying to help the poorer southern laborers.
                   A. Alchian and W. Allen, *University Economics*
    Analysis   The word "profess" here conceals the claim that
northern workers—on the whole—are duplicitous: they say they're
trying to help their southern counterparts when they're really
motivated by self-interest. But the authors have given no reason to
believe that northern workers are not entirely sincere. By noticing
how the authors have used a slanter here, we can be on the alert for
this bias against workers in their book.

2   Arguments

When we try to convince someone that a claim is true because it follows from some other claims, we are making an argument. We need to understand what an argument is and how to evaluate arguments before we can look at any other kind of reasoning.

In Section 2.1 we clarify what an argument is and give the most basic standards for whether an argument is good or bad. This is the most difficult section of the book, but is essential for everything that follows.

Part of determining whether an argument is good is deciding whether the assumptions of an argument are true, which is what we consider in Section 2.2. In Section 2.3 we'll look at how scientists prefer assumptions established by experiment, though nothing later in the text depends on that.

Most arguments we encounter are not complete. But that needn't mean they are bad. We need standards for how to interpret arguments—how to repair them—in order to determine whether we should accept their conclusions. That's what we look at in Section 2.4.

2.1 Arguments

> **Argument** An argument is an attempt to convince someone (possibly yourself) that a particular claim, called the **conclusion**, is true. The rest of the argument is a collection of claims called the **premises**, which are given as the reasons for believing the conclusion is true.
>
> The conclusion is sometimes called the **issue** that is being debated.

Example 1 Critical thinking is the most important subject in school. It will help you reason better, it will help you get a job, and it will help you do better in all your other classes.

Analysis This is an argument. The conclusion is: Critical thinking is the most important subject in school. The premises are: Critical thinking will help you get a job; critical thinking will help you do better in all your other classes.

Example 2 You can tell that economics graduates are smart. They get high-paying jobs, and they always dress well.

Analysis This is an attempt to convince that "Economics graduates are smart" is true. Its premises are "They get high paying jobs" and "They always dress well."

Example 3 (From a label on medication) Follow the directions for using this medicine provided by your doctor. This medicine may be taken on an empty stomach or with food. Store this medicine at room temperature, away from heat and light.

Analysis This is not an argument. Instructions or commands are not an attempt to convince anyone that some claim is true.

Example 4 How come you don't call me? What's wrong? You don't love your mother? Where did I go wrong?

Analysis This is not an argument. Not every attempt to persuade is an attempt to convince that a claim is true.

Certain words can signal to us that a passage should be seen as an argument. An *indicator word* is a word or phrase added to a claim to tell us the role of the claim in an argument or what the speaker thinks about the claim or argument. For example:

Conclusion indicators: hence; therefore; so; thus; consequently; we can then show that; it follows that; . . .

Premise indicators: since; because; for; in as much as; given that; suppose that; it follows from; on account of; due to; . . .

Indicators of speaker's belief: probably; certainly; most likely; I think; . . .

For an argument to be good, it must give us good reason to believe its conclusion is true. But what do we mean by "good reason"?

If we don't have good reason to believe the premises, then they can't provide good reason to believe the conclusion. From a false premise we can derive both a false conclusion and a true conclusion.

Example 5 Lassie is a cat. All cats have fur. So Lassie has fur.
　　Analysis This has a false premise and true conclusion.

Example 6 Lassie is a dog. All dogs can fly. So Lassie can fly.
　　Analysis This has a false premise and a false conclusion.

Plausible claims A claim is plausible if we have good reason to believe it is true. It is less plausible the less reason we have to believe it is true.

An argument is no better than its least plausible premise. But plausible premises are not enough.

Example 7 Dogs have souls. Therefore, you should treat dogs humanely.

Analysis This is a bad argument, because the premise "Dogs have souls" is less plausible than the conclusion. If the premises of an argument are no more plausible than its conclusion, they give us no reason to believe the conclusion.

> **Begging the question**   An argument begs the question if one of its premises is no more plausible than its conclusion.

In a good argument, the premises must also support the conclusion; the conclusion must follow from the premises.

Example 8   You are reading this book. This book was printed in the U.S. Therefore, this book costs less than $30.

Analysis The premises and conclusion of this argument are clearly true, but the premises don't support the conclusion. They give us no reason to believe the conclusion.

Example 9   Dollar bills are printed using green ink. Therefore, U.S. currency is easy to counterfeit.

Analysis Our reaction to the single true premise here is "So?". Why does "U.S. currency is easy to counterfeit" follow from that?

> **Valid argument**   An argument is valid if it is impossible for the premises to be true and the conclusion false (at the same time); otherwise, it is invalid.
>
> **Strong and weak arguments**   Invalid arguments are classified on a scale from strong to weak. An argument is *strong* if it is very unlikely for the premises to be true and the conclusion false (at the same time). An argument is *weak* if it is likely for the premises to be true and the conclusion false (at the same time).
>
> The conclusion *follows from* the premises means that the argument is valid or strong.

Either an argument is valid or it isn't. But
the strength of an invalid argument is a matter of degree.

Example 10 All dogs bark. Ralph is a dog. Therefore,
Ralph barks.
Analysis This is a valid argument. It is impossible for the
premises to be true and the conclusion false at the same time. But
the argument is still bad. The first premise is false: Basenjis can't
bark, some dogs have had their vocal cords cut, ... Whether an
argument is valid or strong depends on the relation between the
premises and conclusion, not on whether the premises actually
happen to be true: *valid ≠ good.*

Example 11 All parakeets anyone I know has ever seen or heard
or read about are under 2 feet tall. Therefore, the parakeets for sale
at the mall are under 2 feet tall.
Analysis This is a strong argument. Surveying all the ways
the premise could be true, we think that yes, a new supergrow bird
food could have been formulated and the parakeets at the local
mall are really 2 feet tall, we just haven't heard about it. Or a rare
giant parakeet from the Amazon forest could have been discovered
and brought here. Or a UFO might have abducted a parakeet by
mistake, hit it with growing rays, and the bird is gigantic. So the
argument is not valid. But all these ways the premise could be true
and the conclusion false are so unlikely that we would have very
good reason to believe the conclusion if the premise is true, even
though the conclusion might be false.

Example 12 Good teachers give fair exams. Dr. E gives fair
exams. So Dr. E is a good teacher.
Analysis This is a weak argument. Dr. E might bore his
students to tears and just copy good exams from the instructor's
manual. Or he might get good exams from another teacher. There
are lots of possibilities that are not unlikely.

Why should we worry whether the conclusion follows
from the premises if we don't know that the premises are
true? Consider what happens when a couple applies for a
home loan. They fill out all the forms and give them to the
loan officer at the bank. She reads their answers. At that

point she might tell them that they don't qualify. That is, even though she doesn't know if the claims they made about their income and assets are true, she can see that even if they are true, the couple won't qualify for a loan. On the other hand, she might tell them that they'll qualify—if those claims are true. Then she'll have to make phone calls, check credit references, and so on, to find out if what they claimed is true. It's the same with arguments: Sometimes it's easier to evaluate first whether an argument is valid or strong in order to find out whether we should bother to investigate whether the premises are true.

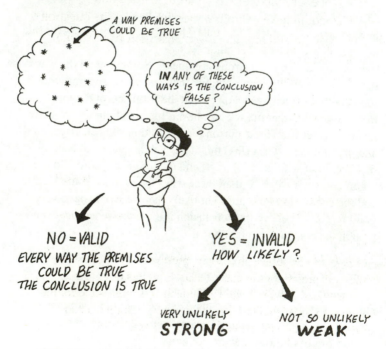

How do we show that an argument is *not* valid or strong? We give an example, some *way* the world might be in which the premises would be true and the conclusion false. *To reason well you must use your imagination.*

Now we can summarize the conditions needed for an argument to be good.

> **Tests for an argument to be good**
> • The premises are plausible.
> • The argument is valid or strong.
> • The premises are more plausible than the conclusion.

Before you proceed further in this book, the following points should be clear:

• Every good argument is valid or strong.
• Not every valid or strong argument is good
  (it could have a dubious premise or beg the question).
• Only invalid arguments are classified from strong
  to weak.
• Every weak argument is bad.
• If the conclusion of a valid argument is false,
  one of the premises must be false.

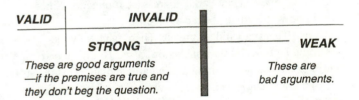

VALID | **INVALID**

STRONG — | — **WEAK**

*These are good arguments
—if the premises are true and
they don't beg the question.*

*These are
bad arguments.*

Example 13 Dr. E is a philosophy professor. All philosophy professors prefer dogs to cats. So Dr. E prefers dogs to cats.
  Analysis This is a valid argument: It is impossible for the premises to be true and the conclusion false. But it's a bad argument, because the second premise is false.

Example 14 Dick is a bachelor. So Dick was never married.
  Analysis This is weak, and hence bad. There is a way that the premise could be true and the conclusion false that is not unlikely: Dick could be divorced.

Example 15 Sandra's hair is naturally brown. Today Sandra's hair is red. So Sandra dyed her hair.

Analysis   Sandra might be taking a new medication that has a strong effect. Or she might have been too close to her car when they were painting it, or . . . . These are ways the premises could be true and the conclusion false, so the argument is not valid. But all these ways are very unlikely, so the argument is strong. If the premises are plausible, it's good.

Example 16   Prosecuting attorney: The defendant intended to kill Louise. He bought a gun three days before he shot her. He practiced shooting at a target that had her name written across it. He staked out her home for two nights. He shot her twice.
Analysis   This is a strong argument. It's good, *if* the premises are plausible.

Example 17   Defendant: I didn't mean to kill Louise. I only wanted to scare her. That's what was in my mind. Only that, I swear.
Analysis   All the defendant is saying may be true, yet the argument is weak, and we have no good reason to believe the conclusion. What he says shouldn't create reasonable doubt.

Example 18   Whenever Spot barks, there's a cat outside. Since he's barking now, there must be a cat outside.
Analysis   This is a valid argument: There is no way the premises could be true and the conclusion false. But it's a bad argument: Perhaps Spot is barking at the garbageman. That doesn't show that the argument is weak—it shows that the first premise is false.

Example 19   All the dockworkers at Boa Vista docks belong to the union. Ralph has been working at Boa Vista docks for two years. So probably Ralph belongs to the union, too.
Analysis   "Probably" is an indicator word about the speaker's belief. The conclusion here is "Ralph belongs to the union," and the argument is valid—regardless of what the speaker thought.

2.2 Evaluating Premises

We need criteria for what counts as good reason to believe an unsupported claim that we might want to use as a premise. But when we don't have good reason to believe a claim, that does not mean we have reason to believe it's false. We might have no evidence that it's true or that it's false, in which case we should suspend judgment.

not believe ≠ believe is false
lack of evidence ≠ evidence it is false

Three choices we can make about whether to believe a claim

- Accept the claim as true.
- Reject the claim as false.
- Suspend judgment.

Here are some criteria we can use to decide when to accept or reject an unsupported claim, listed in order of their importance.

Our most reliable source of information about the world is our own experience.
If you don't trust your own experience, whose experience do you trust? Should you trust your buddy, your spouse, your priest, your professor, the President, the dictator, when what they say contradicts what you know from your own experience?

> Who are you going to believe, me or your own eyes?
> Groucho Marx

Still, claims based on our own experience are no better than our memory and the functioning of our senses at the

19

time of the experience. We reject or don't accept a claim about our own experience if either:

- We have good reason to doubt our memory.
- The claim contradicts other experiences of ours, and there is a good argument (theory) against the claim.

Example 1   The world is flat.

Analysis   Our untutored experience makes it seem that this is true. Nonetheless, we reject it because of other claims we know are true. There is a good theory against the claim.

Example 2   I'm sure I told you to come here Tuesday.

Analysis   Be cautious about arguing with the repairman if you had a bad head cold the day you made an appointment with him.

Example 3   Suzy meets two Chinese students who are good at math and says, "All Chinese students are good at math."

Analysis   All Suzy is justified in claiming is "Two Chinese students are good at math." A claim might seem to be about your own experience, yet it is really a conclusion drawn from your experience.

We can accept a claim made by someone we know and trust who is an authority about that kind of claim.

Example 4   Zoe tells Harry to stay away from the area of town around S. 3rd. She's seen people doing drugs there and knows two people who have been held up in that neighborhood. Zoe is reliable, and her knowledge would matter about these claims.

Example 5   Tom's mother tells him that he should major in business so he can get ahead in life. Should he believe her? She can tell him about her friends' children. But what really are the chances of getting a good job with a degree in business? It would be better to check at the local colleges where they keep records on hiring graduates. He shouldn't reject her claim; he should suspend judgment until he gets more information.

We can accept a claim made by a reputable authority we can trust as an expert on this kind of claim and who has no motive to mislead.

Example 6 Compare:
(a) The Surgeon General announces that smoking is bad for your health.
(b) The doctor hired by the tobacco company says there's no proof that smoking is addictive or causes lung cancer.
(c) The new Surgeon General says that marijuana should be legal.

    Analysis The Surgeon General is a reputable physician with expertise in epidemiology. Further, she's in a position to survey the research on the subject. We have no reason to suspect her motives. So it's reasonable to believe her.

    But is the doctor hired by the tobacco company an expert on smoking-related diseases, or an allergist, or a pediatrician, or . . . . And he has a motive to mislead. No reason to accept his claim.

    Nor is there any reason to accept the Surgeon General's pronouncements about what should be law. Though she's an authority figure, she's not an expert on law and society.

We can accept a claim put forward in a reputable journal or reference source.

Example 7 *The New England Journal of Medicine* is regularly quoted in newspapers, and for good reason. The articles in it are subjected to peer review: Experts in the subject are asked to evaluate whether the research was done to scientific standards. *The National Geographic* has less reliable standards, since they pay for their own research in order to sell their magazine. But it's pretty reliable about natural history. What about the *The Economist*? Are the articles there peer-reviewed or opinion pieces? And anyone can incorporate as the "American Institute for Economic Analysis" or any other title you like. A name is not enough to go by.

We can accept a claim from a media source that is usually reliable and has no obvious motive to mislead, if the person being quoted is named.

It's up to you to decide from experience whether a source is reliable. Don't trust a news report that makes that decision for you by quoting unnamed "usually reliable sources."

They're not even as reliable as the person who's quoting them, and anyway they've covered themselves by saying "usually." *There's never good reason to believe a claim in the media from an unnamed source.* Look also for possible bias in a media source because of its advertisers. Ask yourself, "Who will benefit from my believing this?"

There are no absolute rules for when to accept, when to reject, and when to suspend judgment about a claim. It's a skill, weighing up these criteria, in order of importance.

Criteria for judging unsupported claims

Accept   The claim is known by personal experience.
(Exceptions: Our memory is not good; there's a good argument against our understanding of our experience; it's not our experience at all, but what we've concluded from it.)

Reject   The claim contradicts personal experience.

Reject   The claim contradicts other claims we know to be true.

Accept   The claim is made by someone we know and trust who is an authority about that kind of claim.

Accept   The claim is offered by a reputable authority we can trust as an expert about this kind of claim and who has no motive to mislead.

Accept   The claim is put forward in a reputable journal or reference source.

Accept   The claim is in a media source that's usually reliable and has no obvious motive to mislead, if the original source is named.

We don't have criteria for when to suspend judgment. That's the default attitude we should adopt whenever we don't have good reason to accept or reject a claim.

Advertising Many advertisements are arguments, with the (often unstated) conclusion that you should buy the product, or frequent the establishment, or use the service. Sometimes the claims are accurate. But sometimes they are not. There's nothing special about them, though. They should be judged by the criteria we've already considered. *If you think there should be more stringent criteria for evaluating ads, you're not judging other claims carefully enough.*

The Internet Ask yourself what reason you have to believe something you read on the Internet. Next time you're ready, mouth agape, to swallow what's up there on the screen, imagine your friend saying, "No, really, you believed *that?*" Don't check your brain at the door when you go online.

Above all, remember that personal experience is your best guide. Don't trust others more than yourself about what you know best.

Common mistakes in evaluating unsupported claims

A. *Arguing backwards* It's a mistake to believe the premises of an argument are true just because the argument is valid or strong and the conclusion is true.

Example 8 Your friend says, "All CEOs of computer software companies are rich. Bill Gates is a CEO of a computer software company. So Bill Gates is rich." Since you know that Bill Gates is rich, and the argument is clearly valid, you think it must be that all CEOs of computer software companies are rich.

Analysis This is arguing backwards. There are lots of CEOs of small software companies who are struggling to make a living. An argument is supposed to convince us that its conclusion is true, not that its premises are true.

B. *Appeal to authority* It's a mistake, a bad appeal to authority, to say that we should accept a claim because a particular person said it when that person is not really an authority on the subject or has motive to mislead.

Example 9   —What do you think of the President's new tax plan?
—It must be good, since Dan Rather said so on the TV news.
   Analysis Not everything that Dan Rather says is true.

C. *Mistaking the person (or group) for the claim* It's
often right to suspend judgment on a claim if you don't
consider the person who's making it to be a reputable
authority. But it's never right to say the claim is false
because of who said it.

Example 10 I don't believe the tax cut will benefit the poorest in
our society. That's just another lie our senator said.
   Analysis This mistakes the person for the claim. Politicians
don't lie *all* the time. There's no shortcut for thinking about a
claim in order to evaluate whether to accept it.

Example 11 There's no water shortage here in New Mexico.
That's just one of those things the environmentalists say.
   Analysis This mistakes the group for the claim.

D. *Appeal to common belief* An appeal to common belief
is to accept a claim as true because a lot of other people
believe it. Typically that's a bad appeal to authority.

Example 12 Everyone I know says that Consolidated Computers
is a great investment. So I'm going to buy 500 shares—they can't
all be wrong.
   Analysis This appeal to common belief is just a bad appeal
to authority.

Example 13 Tom goes to England and finds that everyone seems
to be driving on the left-hand side of the road. He concludes that
he should, too.
   Analysis This is good reasoning, since we know that every
country allows driving on just one side.

Similar common mistakes in evaluating arguments

E. *Mistaking the person (or group) for the argument*
It's a mistake to reject an argument as bad just because of
who said it.

Example 14 Zoe: I went to Professor Zzzyzzx's talk about writing last night. He said that the best way to start on a novel is to make an outline of the plot.

Suzy: Are you kidding? He can't even speak English.

Analysis Suzy is mistaking the person for the argument. Professor Zzzyzzx's argument may be good even if Suzy doubts his qualifications to make it.

F. ***Phony refutation*** To *refute* an argument is to show that it is bad. Often we think we can refute an argument by showing that the person who made it doesn't believe one of the premises or even the conclusion itself. But that's a phony refutation: Sincerity of the speaker is not one of the criteria for an argument to be good. Judging by sincerity is just mistaking the person for the argument.

Example 15 Harry: We should stop logging old-growth forests. There are very few of them left in the U.S. They are important watersheds and preserve wildlife. And once cut, we cannot recreate them.

Tom: You say we should stop logging old-growth forests? Who are you kidding? You just built a log cabin on the mountain.

Analysis Tom's rejection of Harry's argument seems reasonable, since Harry's actions betray the conclusion he's arguing for. But whether they do or not (perhaps the logs came from the land Harry's family cleared in a new-growth forest), Tom has not answered Harry's argument. Tom is not justified in ignoring an argument because of Harry's actions.

If Harry were to respond to Tom by saying that the logs for his home weren't cut from an old-growth forest, he's been suckered. Tom got him to change the subject, and they will be deliberating an entirely different claim than he intended. It's a phony refutation.

> *Whether a claim is true or false is not determined by who said it.*
>
> *Whether an argument is good or bad is not determined by who made it.*

2.3 Experiments

The big revolution in science in the Renaissance came when people began looking to their own experience rather than to the ancients for evidence as to how nature works.

An *observational claim* is one that is established either by personal experience or observation in an experiment. Scientists use the word *evidence* to mean the observational claims that are used as premises in an argument. Remember, though, that "personal experience" means reports on what we perceive through our senses—not what we deduce from those perceptions.

What do we mean by "observation in an experiment"? A physicist may say he saw an atom traverse a cloud chamber, when what he actually saw was a line made on a piece of photographic film. A biologist may say she saw the nucleus of a cell, when what she saw was an image projected through a microscope. In both cases these people are not reporting on direct personal experience, but on deductions made from that personal experience. However, those claims made by deduction from the perceptions arising from certain types of experiments are, by consensus in that area of science, deemed to be observations.

Within any one area of science there is a high level of agreement on what counts as an observational claim. But from one area of science to another that standard may vary. A physicist beginning work in biology may well question why certain claims are taken as "obvious" deductions from experience, such as the reality of what you see through a microscope. But after the general form of the inference— from such direct claims about personal experience to the observational claims—is made explicit once or twice, he is likely to accept such claims as undisputed evidence. If he doesn't accept such deductions, he is questioning the basis of that science.

When new techniques are introduced into a science or when a new area of science is developing there is often controversy about what counts as an observational claim. Galileo's report of moons around Jupiter was received with considerable skepticism because telescopes were not assumed to be accurate (indeed, at that time they distorted a lot). In ethology, the study of animal behavior in natural settings, there is not agreement yet on what counts as an observational claim, and you can find different journal articles using different standards.

One constraint we impose on reports of observations is that they should be *reproducible*. That's how we try to avoid subjectivity in science. We believe that nature is uniform. What can happen once can happen again, *if* the conditions are the same. Scientists typically won't accept reports on observations that they don't think can be reproduced.

The difficulty, always, is specifying exactly what conditions are required. It is fairly easy in chemistry and physics; less so in biology; much more difficult in psychology or ethology. It is virtually impossible in history and economics. That would seem to make history and economics not sciences, then, except to the extent that we can describe very general conditions that may recur.

2.4 Repairing Arguments

Example 1 —I heard that Wanda has a pet.
—It must be a dog, 'cause I heard barking in her house yesterday. And I know she doesn't let people bring their pets to her home.
   Analysis This is missing a premise to be a good argument: "Almost any pet that barks is a dog." But why bother saying that? Everyone knows it, and the argument is good enough without it.

   When are we justified in adding or subtracting from an argument without being accused of putting words in someone's mouth? We first need to make some assumptions about people with whom we reason.

The Principle of Rational Discussion We assume that the other person who is discussing with us or whose arguments we are evaluating:
- Knows about the subject under discussion.
- Is able and willing to reason well.
- Is not lying.

   What justification do we have for invoking this principle? Not everyone fits these criteria all the time. But if people don't satisfy the Principle of Rational Discussion, there's no point in reasoning with them.

- If they don't know about the subject, educate, don't debate.

- If they aren't able to reason well, teach them.

- If they aren't willing to reason well, walk away.

- If they're lying, then the only point of reasoning with them is to catch them in their lies.

Above all, it's not worthwhile to reason with someone if he or she is not acting rationally.

> ***The mark of irrationality*** A person is irrational if he or she recognizes that an argument is good but doesn't accept the conclusion.

What if you hear an argument for both sides, and you can't find a flaw in either? Then you should *suspend judgment* on which conclusion is true until you can investigate more.

Still many people don't follow the Principle of Rational Discussion. They don't care if your argument is good. Why not use bad methods of persuasion? Why should we follow these rules and assume them of others? If you don't:

- You are denying the essentials of democracy.
- You are likely to undermine your own ability to evaluate arguments.
- You are not as likely to convince others.

If you once forfeit the confidence of your fellow citizens, you can never regain their respect and esteem. It is true that you may fool all the people some of the time; you can even fool some of the people all the time; but you cannot fool all of the people all the time.
                                                Abraham Lincoln

With the Principle of Rational Discussion, we can formulate a guide to help us in evaluating arguments. Since the person is supposed to be able to reason well, we can add a premise only if it makes the argument stronger or valid and doesn't beg the question. Since the person isn't lying and knows the subject under discussion, any premise we add should be plausible, and plausible to the other person. We can also delete a premise if doing so doesn't make the argument any worse. A premise is ***irrelevant*** if you can delete it and the argument isn't any weaker.

Guide to repairing arguments Given an (implicit) argument that is apparently defective, we are justified in *adding* a premise or conclusion if:

1. The argument becomes stronger or valid.
2. The premise is plausible and would seem plausible to the other person.
3. The premise is more plausible than the conclusion.

If the argument is then valid or strong yet one of the original premises is false or dubious, we may *delete* that premise if the argument remains valid or strong.

We don't need to know what the speaker was thinking in order to find a claim that makes the argument strong or valid, so we take (1) to have priority over (2). By first trying to make the argument valid or strong, we show the other person what he or she needs to assume to make the argument good.

Sometimes it's clear that an argument is bad and there's no point in trying to repair it. Here are criteria for when we can write off an argument as unrepairable.

Unrepairable arguments We can't repair an argument if any one of the following hold:

• There's no argument there.
• The argument is so lacking in coherence that there's nothing obvious to add.
• The premises it uses are false or very dubious and cannot be deleted.
• The obvious premise to add would make the argument weak.
• The obvious premise to add to make the argument strong or valid is false.
• The conclusion is clearly false.

But remember: *When you show that an argument is bad, you have not proved that the conclusion is false.*

Example 2 No dog meows. So Spot does not meow.

Analysis "Spot is a dog" is the only premise that will make this a valid or strong argument. So we add that. Then, if this new claim is true, the argument is good. We don't add "Spot barks." That's true and may seem obvious to the person who stated the argument, but it doesn't make the argument any better. So adding it violates (1) of the Guide. *We repair only as needed.*

Example 3 All MBAs have at least five years of post-secondary education. So Lisa is an MBA.

Analysis The obvious premise to add is "Lisa has at least five years of post-secondary education." But then the argument is still weak (Lisa could be a doctor, or a mathematician, or . . .). *If the obvious premise to add makes the argument weak, the argument is unrepairable.*

Example 4 Dr. E is a good teacher because he gives fair exams.

Analysis The unstated premise needed here is "Almost any teacher who gives fair exams is a good teacher." That gives a strong argument. But it's dubious, since a bad teacher could copy fair exams from the instructor's manual. (If you thought "Good teachers give fair exams" would do, reread Example 9, p. 15.) *The argument can't be repaired because the obvious premise to add to make the argument strong or valid is false or dubious.*

But can't we make it strong by adding, say, "Dr. E gives great explanations," "Dr. E is amusing," "Dr. E never misses class," . . .? Yes, all those are true, and perhaps obvious to the person. But adding them doesn't repair this argument. It makes a whole new argument. *Don't put words in someone's mouth.*

Example 5 You can tell that economics graduates are smart. They get high-paying jobs, and they always dress well.

Analysis The argument is weak—and it *is* an argument: The last sentence is meant as evidence. But there's no obvious repair to the argument, as it's false that anyone who gets a high-paying job and dresses well is smart. *The person apparently can't reason.*

Example 6 You shouldn't eat the fat on your steak. Haven't you heard that cholesterol is bad for you?

Analysis The conclusion is the first sentence. But what are the premises? The speaker's question is rhetorical, meant to be taken as an assertion: "Cholesterol is bad for you." But that alone won't give us the conclusion. We need something like "Steak fat has a lot of cholesterol" and "You shouldn't eat anything that's bad for you." Premises like these are so obvious we don't bother to say them. This argument is O.K.

Example 7 You're going to vote for the Green Party candidate for President? Don't you realize that means your vote will be wasted?

Analysis Here, too, the questions are rhetorical, meant to be taken as assertions: "Don't vote for the Green Party candidate" (the conclusion) and "Your vote will be wasted" (the premise). This sounds reasonable, though something is missing. A visitor from Denmark may not know that "The Green Party candidate doesn't have a chance of winning" is true. But she may also question why that matters. We'd have to fill in the argument further: "If you vote for someone who doesn't have a chance of winning, then your vote will be wasted." And when we add that premise we see the argument that used such "obvious" premises is really not very good. Why should we believe that if you vote for someone who doesn't stand a chance of winning then your vote is wasted? If that were true, then who wins is the only important result of an election, rather than, say, making a position understood by the electorate. At best we can say that when the unstated premises are added in, we get an argument one of whose premises needs a substantial argument to convince us that it is true. *Trying to repair arguments can lead us to unstated assumptions about which the real debate should be.*

Example 8 Cats are more likely than dogs to carry diseases harmful to humans. Cats kill songbirds and can kill people's pets. Cats disturb people at night with their screeching and clattering in garbage cans. Cats leave paw prints on cars and will sleep in unattended cars. Cats are not as pleasant as dogs and are owned only by people who have satanic affinities. So there should be a leash law for cats just as much as for dogs.

Analysis This letter to the editor is going pretty well until the next to last sentence. *That claim is a bit dubious, and the argument would be just as strong without it. So we should delete it.*

Then we have an argument which, with some unstated premises you can supply, is pretty good.

Example 9 In a famous speech, Martin Luther King Jr. said:

I have a dream that one day this nation will rise up and live out the true meaning of its creed: "We hold these truths to be self-evident—that all men are created equal." . . . I have a dream that one day even the state of Mississippi, a desert state sweltering with the heat of injustice and oppression, will be transformed into an oasis of freedom and justice. I have a dream that my four little children will one day live in a nation where they will not be judged by the color of their skin but by the content of their character.

. . . King is also presenting a logical argument . . . the argument might be stated as follows; "America was founded on the principle that all men are created equal. This implies that people should not be judged by skin color, which is an accident of birth, but rather by what they make of themselves ('the content of their character'). To be consistent with this principle, America should treat black people and white people alike. *The Art of Reasoning,* David Kelley

Analysis The rewriting of this passage is too much of a stretch—putting words in someone's mouth—to be appropriate. Where did David Kelley get the premise "This implies . . ."? Stating my dreams and hoping others will share them is not an argument. Martin Luther King, Jr. knew how to argue well and could do so when he wanted. We're not going to make his words more respectable by pretending they're an argument. *Not every good attempt to persuade is an argument.*

Example 10 Environmentalists should not be allowed to tell us what to do. The federal government should not be allowed to tell us what to do. Therefore, we should go ahead and allow logging in old-growth forests.

Analysis The speaker has confused whether we have the right to cut down forests with whether we should cut them down. The argument is weak; indeed, we could delete either premise and it wouldn't be any weaker. *The speaker's premises are irrelevant to the conclusion.*

Example 11   U.S. citizens are independent souls, and they tend to dislike being forced to do anything. The compulsory nature of Social Security therefore has been controversial since the program's beginnings. Many conservatives argue that Social Security should be made voluntary, rather than compulsory.

J. M. Brux and J. L. Cowen, *Economic Issues and Policy*

Analysis   The first two sentences look like an argument. But the first sentence is too vague to be a claim, and there's no obvious way to make it precise. So *we can't view this as an argument*, and there's certainly no repair for it.

Example 12   (1) Investors in 1997 invested more than twice as much money in no-load mutual funds as in other mutual funds. So, (2) Investors in 1997 overwhelmingly preferred no-load mutual funds.

Analysis   Typically, we invoke some evidence such as (1), which is objective, to conclude (2), which is subjective. But to have a good argument for (2) we also need a premise like "When someone invests money in a fund, they prefer that fund to one that they do not invest in," which is plausible and makes this a good argument. That subjective claim is the link between the observed behavior and the inferred state of mind. Often *an unstated assumption linking behavior to thoughts is needed to make an argument good.*

When someone leaves a conclusion unsaid, he or she is *implying* the conclusion. When you decide that an unstated claim is the conclusion, you are *inferring* that claim. We also say that someone is implying a claim if in context it's clear that he or she believes the claim. In that case we infer that the person believes the claim.

Example 13   I'm not going to vote, because no matter who becomes mayor, nothing is going to get done to repair roads in this part of town.

Analysis   An unstated claim is needed to make sense of what is said: "If no matter who becomes mayor nothing is going to get done to repair roads in this part of town, then you shouldn't vote for mayor." We infer this from the person's remarks; he or she has implied it.

2.5 Fallacies

We have criteria for when an argument is unrepairable.
In addition, there are certain kinds of arguments that
throughout this text we will pick out as being unrepairable.

> **Fallacy** A fallacy is a bad argument of one of the types
> that have been agreed to be typically unrepairable.

Some kinds of fallacies are identifiable by virtue of their
using or requiring a premise that is normally false. We've
seen two of those already. A drawing the line fallacy
requires as premise "If you can't make the difference precise,
then there is no difference." A subjectivist fallacy requires
"There is a lot of disagreement about whether this claim is
true, and if there is so much disagreement, then the claim is
subjective."

Other fallacies, such as shifting the burden of proof or
begging the question, violate the Principle of Rational
Discussion.

Still others are bad because of their structure relative to
certain words, such as "if . . . then . . ." or "all," as we'll see
in Chapter 3.

One type of fallacy we'll look at here are arguments that
depend on too much emotion. Emotions do and should play a
role in our reasoning: We cannot even begin to make good
decisions if we don't consider their significance in our
emotional life. But that does not mean we should be swayed
entirely by our emotions.

An *appeal to emotion* in an argument is a premise that
says, roughly, you should believe or do something because
you feel a certain way. Often we call the entire argument an
appeal to emotion.

Example 1 —You should vote for Ralph for school president.
—Why?
—Because he doesn't have many friends.
Analysis To construe this as a strong or valid argument, we
need to add "You should vote for someone you feel sorry for."
That's an *appeal to pity*, and in this case is implausible.

Example 2 (Dick to Zoe) We should give to the American
Friends Service Committee. They help people all over the world
help themselves, and they don't ask those they help whether they
agree with them. They've been doing it well for nearly a century
now, and they have very low overhead: almost all the money they
get is given to those who are in need. All those people who don't
have running water or health care deserve our help. Think of those
poor kids growing up malnourished and sick. We've got enough
money to send them at least $50.
Analysis This requires an unstated premise appealing to pity,
too. But it isn't just "Do it because you feel sorry for someone."
What's needed is something like "If you feel sorry for people, *and*
you have a way to help them that is efficient and morally upright,
and you have enough money to help, then you should send the
organization money." That seems plausible, though whether it is
the best use of Zoe and Dick's money needs to be addressed.

Example 3 You shouldn't drive so quickly in the rain. The roads
are very slippery after the first rain of the season and we could get
into an accident.
Analysis Normally an appeal to emotion by itself is not
sufficient to make a good argument. But not always. Sometimes
an *appeal to fear*, as in this example, can be the sole legitimate
factor in making a decision. An appeal to emotion that concludes
you should *do* something can be good or it can be bad.

Example 4 This diet will work because I have to lose 20 pounds
by the end of the month for Marjorie's wedding.
Analysis This is an example of *wishful thinking*, and it's
bad. *An appeal to emotion whose conclusion is a description
of the world is bad*, if the appeal cannot be deleted as a premise.
Why should we believe some description is true just because we
are moved by our emotions? Wishing it so doesn't make it so.

2.6 Counterarguments

Raising objections and answering them is part of making and evaluating arguments.

Example 1 Dick: Zoe, we ought to get another dog.
Zoe: What's wrong with Spot?
Dick: Oh, no, I mean to keep Spot company.
Zoe: Spot has us. He doesn't need company.
Dick: But we're gone a lot. And he's always escaping from the yard, 'cause he's lonely. And we don't give him enough time. He should be out running around more.
Zoe: But think of all the work! We'll have to feed the new dog. And think of all the time necessary to train it.
Dick: I'll train him. We can feed him at the same time as Spot, and dog food is cheap. It won't cost much.

Dick is trying to convince Zoe to believe "We should get another dog." But he has to answer her objections.

We ought to get another dog.
   (*objection*) We already have Spot.
The other dog will keep Spot company. (*answer*)
   (*objection*) Spot already has us for company.
We are gone a lot. (*answer*)
He is always escaping from the yard. (*answer*)
He's lonely. (*answer*)
We don't give him enough time. (*answer*)
He should be out running around more. (*answer*)
   (*objection*) It will be a lot of work to have a new dog.
   (*objection*) We will have to feed the new dog.
   (*objection*) It will take a lot of time to train the new dog.
I (Dick) will train him. (*answer*)
We can feed him at the same time as Spot. (*answer*)
Dog food is cheap. (*answer*)

Argument. Counterargument. Counter-counterargument. Objections are raised: Someone puts forward a claim that, if true, makes one of our claims false or at least doubtful. We then have to answer that challenge to sustain our argument. *Knocking off an objection is a mini-argument within your argument—if it's not a good (though brief) argument, it won't do the job.*

But reasoning well doesn't mean you always "win." You could say to an objection, "I hadn't thought of that, I guess you're right." Or you could say, "I don't know, I'll have to think about that."

In making an argument, you'll want to make it strong. You might think you have a great one. All the premises seem obvious and they lead to the conclusion. But if you imagine someone objecting, you can see how to give better support for doubtful premises or make it clearer that the argument is valid or strong. And answering counterarguments in your own writing allows the reader to see you haven't ignored some obvious objections. Just make a list of the pros and cons. Then answer the other side.

All the ways we can show an argument is unrepairable are useful in refuting an argument. Three are fundamental.

Direct ways of refuting an argument
- Show that at least one of the premises is false.
- Show that the argument isn't valid or strong.
- Show that the conclusion is false.

Example 2 It's useless to kill flies. The ones you kill will be the slowest, because the fastest ones will evade you. Over time, then, the genes for being fast will predominate. Then with super-fast flies, it will be impossible to kill them anyway. So it's useless to kill flies.

To refute this argument: We might object to one of the premises, saying that you won't be killing the slowest ones, but only the ones that happen to come into your house.

Or we might accept the premises, but note that "over time" could be thousands of years, so the conclusion doesn't follow.

Or we could attack the conclusion directly, pointing out that we kill flies all the time and it keeps the house clean.

We can also refute an argument in an *indirect way*. Recall that if a valid argument has a false conclusion, one of the premises is false. If a strong argument has a false conclusion, one of the premises is very likely false. And if the conclusion is absurd, the premises aren't what you want.

> ***Reducing to the absurd***   To reduce to the absurd is to show that at least one of several claims is false or dubious, or collectively they are unacceptable, by drawing a false or unwanted conclusion from them.

Example 3 You complain that taxes are already too high and there is too much crime. And you say we should permanently lock up everyone who has been convicted of three felonies. In the places where this has been instituted it hasn't reduced the crime rate. So we will have many, many more people who will be incarcerated for their entire lives. We will need more prisons, many more, because these people will be in forever. We will need to employ more guards. We will need to pay for a lot of health care for these people when they are elderly. Thus, if you lock up everyone who has been convicted of three felonies, we will have to pay substantially higher taxes. Since you are adamant that taxes are too high, you should abandon your claim that we should permanently lock up everyone who has been convicted of three felonies.

Analysis Here the speaker is showing that the claims that taxes are too high and that we should lock up everyone who has been convicted of three felonies lead to a contradiction.

When you use this method, be sure that the argument you use to get the false or absurd conclusion is good. Otherwise it may be the claims you introduce or the weakness of the argument you make that give the contradiction.

One way to reduce to the absurd is to use similar premises in an argument that sounds just like the original, yet leads to an absurd conclusion. This is refuting by analogy (see pp. 67–68).

Example 4   Look, your argument against killing flies is bad. We could use the same argument against killing bacteria, or against killing chickens for dinner from a farmer's henhouse. Those conclusions would be absurd.

There are several ways to try to refute that are bad. We've seen *slippery slope arguments* and *phony refutations*. In addition, there is the worthless method of **ridicule**, which ends a discussion, belittles others, and makes enemies.

Example 5   Dr. E: I hear that your department elected a woman as chairman.

Professor Smythe: Yes, indeed. And now we're trying to decide what we should call her—"chairman" or "chairwoman" or "chairperson."

Dr. E: "Chairperson"? Why not use a neutral term that's really appropriate for the position, like "chaircreature"?

Analysis   No argument has been given for why "chairman" shouldn't be replaced by "chairperson," although Dr. E thinks he's shown that the idea is ridiculous.

Finally, there is the all-purpose way to evade another person's argument. A *strawman* is a bad way to refute by putting words in someone's mouth.

Example 6   Tom: Unless we allow the logging of old-growth forests in this county, we'll lose the timber industry and these towns will die.

Dick: So you're saying that you don't care what happens to the spotted owl and to our rivers and the water we drink?

Tom: I said nothing of the sort. You've misrepresented my position.

Analysis   The only reasonable response to a strawman is to say calmly, "That isn't what I said."

3 Reasoning with Special Kinds of Claims

Certain kinds of claims require special skills to analyze in arguments.

In Section 3.1 we look at claims made from other claims using the words "or" and "not." Then we'll consider how to reason with compound claims that use "if . . . then . . .", which are essential for reasoning about hypothetical situations. We'll learn how to recognize specific kinds of arguments as valid or weak by inspecting their form with respect to those words. We'll also see how to form the contradictory of a claim and how to analyze claims that talk about necessary and sufficient conditions.

In Section 3.2 we look at claims about some portion of a collection, whether all, or some, almost all, or a very few. We need to be aware of typical mistakes and typical good arguments that use these kinds of general claims.

Of special importance are claims that state what we think should or should not be, based on some value judgment. We'll study those in Section 3.3.

3.1 Compound Claims

> **Compound claim** A compound claim is one that is composed of other claims but has to be viewed as just one claim.

Example 1 Either a Democrat will win the election or a Republican will win the election.

    Analysis This is a compound claim composed of the claims "A democrat will win the election" and "A Republican will win the election" joined by the word "or." Whether it is true or false depends on whether one or both of its parts are true.

Example 2 Suzy will pass her exam because she studied so hard.

    Analysis This is not a compound claim. "Because" is an indicator word showing that this is an argument.

We call the claims that make up an "or" claim the **alternatives**.

Example 3 Dick or Zoe will go to the grocery to get eggs.

    Analysis We can view this as an "or" claim with alternatives "Dick will go to the grocery to get eggs" and "Zoe will go to the grocery to get eggs."

Essential to reasoning well is knowing how to disagree, how to assert the opposite of what someone else has said.

> **Contradictory of a claim** A contradictory of a claim is one that must have the opposite truth-value.

Example 4 Spot is barking.

    Analysis A contradictory is "Spot is not barking."

Example 5 Inflation will be not be less than 3% this year.

Analysis We can contradict this by saying "Inflation will be less than 3% this year," which doesn't contain "not," or we can contradict it by saying "Inflation will be 3% or less this year."

In order to discuss contradictories and some valid arguments that depend on the forms of claims, we'll use the following conventions in discussions and diagrams:

The letters A, B, and C stand for any claims.

We write "not A" as short for "a contradictory of A."

An arrow (➞) stands for "therefore."

The symbol "+" means an additional premise.

Contradictory of an "or" claim
A or B has contradictory *not A and not B*.
Contradictory of an "and" claim
A and B has contradictory *not A or not B*.

Example 6 Maria got the van or Manuel won't go to school.
  Analysis A contradictory is "Maria didn't get the van, and Manuel will go to school."

Example 7 Tom or Suzy will pick up Manuel for class today.
  Analysis A contradictory is "Neither Tom nor Suzy will pick up Manuel for class today." We also use "neither . . . nor . . ." for contradictories of "or" claims.

Here a type of argument whose validity we can recognize from just its form.

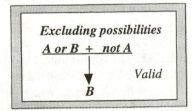

Excluding possibilities
<u>*A or B* + *not A*</u>

Valid

B

Example 8 Either there is a wheelchair ramp at the school dance, or Manuel stayed home. But there isn't a wheelchair ramp at the school dance. So Manuel stayed home.

Analysis This is a valid argument: There is no way that the premises could be true and the conclusion false.

We can reason equally well with more than two alternatives: "A or B or C; not A; not B; therefore C" is valid, too. Or we can exclude just some of the possibilities.

Example 9 Either all criminals should be locked up forever, or we should put more money into rehabilitating criminals, or we should accept that our streets will never be safe, or we should have some system for monitoring ex-convicts. (*This is all one claim*: A or B or C or D.) We can't lock up all criminals forever, because it would be too expensive. We definitely won't accept that our streets will never be safe. So either we should put more money into rehabilitating criminals, or we should have some system for monitoring ex-convicts.

Though reasoning by excluding possibilities is valid, it may not be good. A *false dilemma* is a bad use of excluding possibilities where the "or" claim is false or dubious. Sometimes just the dubious "or" claim is called a "false dilemma."

Example 10 Zoe: Look at these bills! You're either going to have to quit buying those nasty expensive cigars or get rid of Spot.
    Dick: What are you talking about? We can't get rid of Spot.
    Zoe: So you agree, you'll give up smoking those cigars.
    Analysis Zoe poses a false dilemma. They could economize by not dining out.

Example 11 Society can choose high environmental quality but only at the cost of lower tourism or more tourism and commercialization at the expense of the ecosystem, but society must choose. It involves a tradeoff.   R. Sexton, *Exploring Economics*
    Analysis This is a false dilemma: The alternatives are claimed to be mutually exclusive. But Costa Rica has created a lot of tourism by preserving almost 50% of its land in parks. When you see a *versus*-claim, think "Is this a false dilemma?"

Conditional claims are how we reason about possibilities.

> **Conditional claim** A claim that is or can be rewritten as an "if . . . then . . ." claim that must have the same truth-value.
>
> **Antecedent and consequent** In a conditional (rewritten as) "If A, then B," the claim A is the *antecedent*, and the claim B is the *consequent*.

Example 12 If Spot ran away, then the gate was left open.
    Analysis This is a conditional, with antecedent "Spot ran away" and consequent "The gate was left open." The consequent need not happen later.

Example 13 I'll never talk to you again if you don't apologize.
    Analysis This is a conditional with antecedent "You don't apologize" and consequent "I'll never talk to you again."

Example 14 Bring me an ice cream cone and I'll be happy.
    Analysis This is a conditional with antecedent "You bring me an ice cream cone" and consequent "I'll be happy."

Example 15 Loving someone means you never throw dishes at them.
    Analysis This is a conditional with antecedent "You love someone" and consequent "You never throw dishes at them."

Example 16 If Dick goes to the basketball game, then either he got a free ticket or he borrowed money for one.
    Analysis This is a conditional whose consequent is another compound claim.

Example 17 A claim is compound if it is made up of other claims.
    Analysis This is not a conditional, nor a compound. The word "if" is used here to make a definition.

> **Contradictory of a conditional**
> *If A, then B* has contradictory *A, but not B*.

A contradictory of a conditional is not another conditional.

Example 18 If Spot barks, then Flo's cat will run away.
Contradictory: Spot barked, but Flo's cat did not run away.

Example 19 If Spot got out of the yard, he was chasing a squirrel.
Contradictory: Spot got out of the yard, but he wasn't chasing a squirrel.

Example 20 If cats had no fur, they wouldn't give people allergies.
Contradictory: Even if cats had no fur, they would still give people allergies. "Even if" is often used to make a contradictory where there's a false antecedent. The "if" in it does not create a conditional.

Example 21 Bring me an ice cream cone and I'll be happy.
Contradictory: Despite that you brought me an ice cream cone, I'm not happy. "Despite that" is also used to make a contradictory.

Example 22 (†) If Suzy handed in all her homework in English, then she passed the course.
Analysis A contradictory is "Suzy handed in all her homework in English, but she didn't pass the course." The following are not contradictories:

"If Suzy didn't hand in all her homework in English, then she passed the course." (Both this and † could be true if Suzy passed regardless.)

"If Suzy handed in all her homework in English, then she didn't pass the course." (Both this and † could be true by default if Suzy didn't hand in all her homework.)

"If Suzy didn't hand in all her homework, then she didn't pass the course." (Both this and † could be true.)

Contrapositive   The contrapositive of *If A, then B* is *If not B, then not A.* The contrapositive is true exactly when the original conditional is true.

Example 23 If Zoe does the dishes, then Dick will walk Spot.

Contrapositive: If Dick doesn't walk Spot, then Zoe didn't do the dishes.

Note that "only if" does not mean the same as "if."

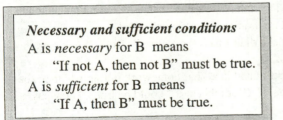

"Only if" *A only if B* means
the same as *If not B, then not A.*

Example 24 Dick will go into the army only if there is a draft.

Analysis This example means the same as: If there is no draft, then Dick will not go into the army.

Example 25 The following are equivalent:

"You can get a speeding ticket only if you are going over the speed limit."

"If you don't go over the speed limit, then you won't get a speeding ticket."

"If you get a speeding ticket, then you went over the speed limit."

Necessary and sufficient conditions
A is *necessary* for B means
  "If not A, then not B" must be true.
A is *sufficient* for B means
  "If A, then B" must be true.

Example 26 Passing an eye test is necessary but not sufficient for getting a driver's license.

Analysis This means "If you don't pass an eye test, you can't get a driver's license" is always true; but "If you pass an eye test, you get a driver's license" need not be true.

Example 27 You can pass calculus only if you study hard.

Analysis This isn't the same as "If you study hard, you can pass calculus." Rather, studying hard is necessary, required to pass calculus. It's not sufficient. The example is equivalent to "If you pass calculus, you studied hard." Confusing "only if" with "if" is confusing necessary with sufficient conditions.

There are some simple valid forms of reasoning using conditionals that are useful for analyzing and making arguments. There are also some very similar looking arguments that are usually weak. To give examples, suppose all the conditionals in the picture below are true.

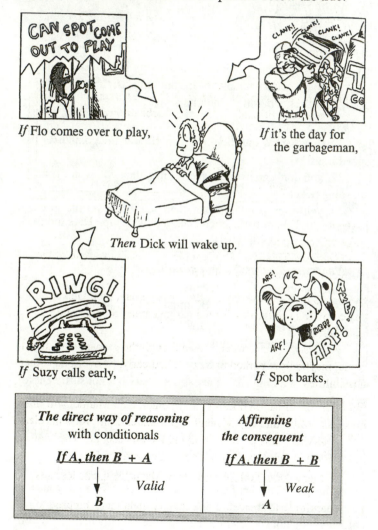

If Flo comes over to play,

If it's the day for the garbageman,

Then Dick will wake up.

If Suzy calls early,

If Spot barks,

The direct way of reasoning with conditionals	**Affirming** **the consequent**
<u>*If A, then B* + *A*</u>	<u>*If A, then B* + *B*</u>
↓ *Valid*	↓ *Weak*
B	*A*

Example 28 If Spot barks, then Dick will wake up. Spot barked. So Dick woke up.

Analysis This is a valid argument. It is impossible for both the premises to be true and the conclusion false. It's an example of the direct way of reasoning with conditionals.

Example 29 If Spot barks, then Dick will wake up. Dick woke up. So Spot barked.

    Analysis This is weak. Maybe Suzy called, or Flo came over to play. It's *reasoning backwards*, an example of affirming the consequent.

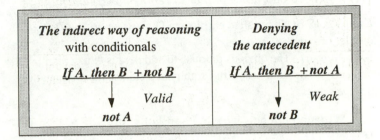

Example 30 If Spot barks, then Dick will wake up. Dick didn't wake up. So Spot didn't bark.

    Analysis This is a valid argument. It is an example of the indirect way of reasoning with conditionals.

Example 31 If it's the day for the garbageman, then Dick will wake up. It's not the day for the garbageman. So Dick didn't wake up.

    Analysis This is weak. Even though the garbageman didn't come, maybe Spot barked or Suzy called early. It overlooks other possibilities.

Example 32 If Maria doesn't call Manuel, then Manuel will miss his class. Maria did call Manuel. So Manuel didn't miss his class.

    Analysis This is weak, denying the antecedent. The "not" in the form indicates a contradictory. Schematically:

    If <u>Maria doesn't call Manuel</u>, *then* <u>Manuel will miss his class</u>.
            A   B

    <u>Maria did call Manuel</u>.   *So* <u>Manuel didn't miss his class</u>.
      not A   not B

Example 33 If Suzy doesn't call early, then Zoe won't go shopping. Zoe went shopping. So Suzy called early.

Analysis This is valid, an example of the indirect way. Here the contradictories don't use "not."

Example 34 Zoe won't go shopping if Dick comes home early. Zoe went shopping. So Dick didn't come home early.

Analysis This is valid, another example of the indirect way.

These invalid forms of arguing are obvious confusions with valid forms, mistakes a good reasoner doesn't make. When you see one, *don't bother to repair the argument.*

Example 35 If Suzy called early, then Dick woke up. So Dick didn't wake up.

Analysis The obvious premise to add here is "Suzy didn't call early." But that makes the argument weak, so the argument is unrepairable.

With conditionals we can go little by little: If A, then B; If B, then C; .... . Then if A is true, we can conclude the last consequent.

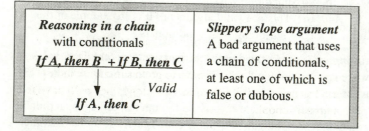

Reasoning in a chain with conditionals $\underline{If\,A,\,then\,B}$ + $\underline{If\,B,\,then\,C}$ $\downarrow$ *Valid* *If A, then C*	*Slippery slope argument* A bad argument that uses a chain of conditionals, at least one of which is false or dubious.

Example 36 If Dick takes Spot for a walk, then Zoe will cook dinner. And if Zoe cooks dinner, then Dick will do the dishes. So if Dick takes Spot for a walk, then he'll do the dishes. But Dick did take Spot for a walk. So he must have done the dishes.

Analysis This is a valid argument, reasoning in a chain with conditionals, where we conclude the last consequent. It's good if all the premises are true.

Example 37 Don't get a credit card! If you do, you'll be tempted to spend money you don't have. Then you'll max out on your card. Then you'll be in real debt. And you'll have to drop out of school to pay your bills. You'll end up a failure in life.

Analysis This is a slippery slope argument, which you can see by rewriting it using conditionals.

Often when we reason about possibilities, we're not sure if they're true, but we want to see what follows from them.

Reasoning from hypotheses The following are equivalent:
- Start with an hypothesis A and make a good argument for B.
- Make a good argument for "If A, then B."

Example 38 Lee: I'm thinking of majoring in biology.

Maria: That means you'll take summer school. Here's why: You're in your second year now. To finish in four years like you told me you need to, you'll have to take all the upper-division biology courses your last two years. And you can't take any of those until you've finished the three-semester calculus course. So you'll have to take calculus over the summer in order to finish in four years.

Analysis Maria has not proved that Lee has to go to summer school. Rather, on the assumption (hypothesis) that Lee will major in biology, Lee will have to go to summer school. That is, Maria has proved: If Lee majors in biology, then he'll have to go to summer school.

3.2 General Claims

General claims are ones that make assertions about some part of a collection.

All means "Every single one, no exceptions."
Sometimes *all* is meant as "Every single one, and there is at least one."
Some means "At least one."
Sometimes *some* is meant as "At least one, but not all."

Which of these readings is best depends on how the words are used in an argument.

Example 1 All dogs are mammals.
   Analysis This is a true claim.

Example 2 All bank managers are women.
   Analysis This is a false claim, on either reading of "all."

Example 3 All polar bears in Antarctica can swim.
   Analysis This is a true claim if you understand "all" as "every single one." It is false if you understand "all" to mean also "at least one," since there aren't any polar bears in Antarctica.

Example 4 Some dogs bark.
   Analysis This is true on either reading of "some."

Example 5 Some dogs are mammals.
   Analysis This is true if you understand "some" to mean "at least one." But it is false if you understand "some" to include "and not all."

There are many different ways to say "all" in English. For example, the following are equivalent claims:

All dogs bark.	Dogs bark.
Every dog barks.	Everything that's a dog barks.

There are also many ways to say the first reading of "some" in English. The following are all equivalent:

Some dogs can't bark.   At least one dog can't bark.
There is a dog that can't bark.   There exists a dog that can't bark.

And there are many ways to say that *nothing* or *none* of a collection satisfies some condition. For example, the following are equivalent claims:

No dog likes cats.   Nothing that's a dog likes cats.
All dogs do not like cats.   Not even one dog likes cats.

Just as we had to be careful with "only if," we need to take care with reasoning with "only."

Example 6 Only bank employees can open the vault at this bank. Pete is a bank employee here. So Pete can open the vault.
   Analysis The premises may be true, but the conclusion could be false: Pete might be the janitor. "Only" does not mean "all." "Only bank employees can open the vault" means "Anyone who can open the vault is a bank employee."

"*Only*" claims   *Only S are P* means *All P are S.*

Here are examples of contradictories of general claims.

Example 7 All people want to be rich.
   Contradictory Some people don't want to be rich.

Example 8 Some Russians like chili.
   Contradictory No Russian likes chili.

Example 9 Some women don't want to marry.
   Contradictory All women want to marry.

Example 10 No women are truck drivers.
   Contradictory Some women are truck drivers.

Example 11 Every Mexican likes vodka.
   Contradictory Some Mexicans don't like vodka.

Example 12 Some whales eat fish.
Contradictory Not even one whale eats fish.

Example 13 Only dogs bark.
Contradictory Some things that bark are not dogs.
To say that just exactly dogs bark and nothing else, we could say "Dogs and only dogs bark." The contradictory of that is "Either some dogs don't bark, or some things that bark aren't dogs."

Given the many ways to make general claims, we have only a rough guide for how to form their contradictories.

Claim	Contradictory
All S are P	Some S are not P Not every S is P
Some S are P	No S are P All S are not P Not even one S is P
Some S are not P	All S are P
No S is P	Some S are P
Only S are P	Some P are not S Not every P is S

There are several methods that can help you determine whether an argument using general claims is valid or weak, which we describe in our textbook *Critical Thinking*. Here we'll just contrast the most common valid forms with similar forms of arguments that are weak.

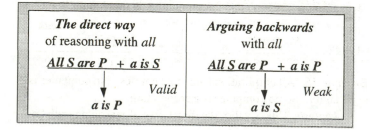

Example 14 All accountants are honest. Ralph is an accountant.
So Ralph is honest.

Analysis This is valid, an example of the direct way of
reasoning with "all." But though valid, it's not good: the first
premise is false, as we learned with Enron.

Example 15 All doctors earn more than $50,000. Earl earns
more than $50,000. So Earl is a doctor.

Analysis This is weak, arguing backwards with "all." Earl
could be a basketball player or an accountant.

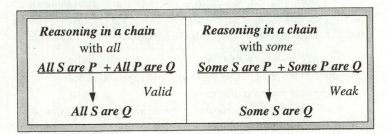

Example 16 Every newspaper that the Vice-President reads is
published by an American publisher. All newspapers published by
an American publisher are biased against Muslims. So the Vice-
President reads only newspapers that are biased against Muslims.

Analysis This is valid, reasoning in a chain with "all."

Example 17 Some dogs like peanut butter. Some things that like
peanut butter are human. So some dogs are human.

Analysis This is weak, reasoning in a chain with "some."

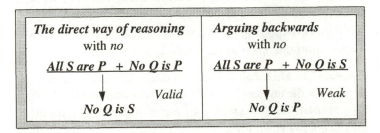

Example 18 All corporations are legal entities. No computer is a
legal entity. So no computer is a corporation.

Analysis This is valid, the direct way of reasoning with "no."

Example 19   All nursing students take critical thinking in their freshman year. No heroin addict is a nursing student. So no heroin addict takes critical thinking his or her freshman year.

Analysis   This is weak, arguing backwards with "no."

Precise generalities are easy to evaluate in arguments.

Example 20   72% of all workers at the GM plant say they will vote to strike. Harry works at the GM plant. So Harry will vote to strike.

Analysis   We can say exactly where this argument lands on the strong-weak scale: There's a 28% chance the premises could be true and the conclusion false. That's not good enough to be strong.

Example 21   95% plus-or-minus 2% of all cat owners have cat-induced allergies. Dr. E's ex-wife has a cat. So Dr. E's ex-wife has cat-induced allergies.

Analysis   This is a strong argument, and it's good if the premises are true.

Example 22   Only 4% of all workers on the assembly line at the GM plant didn't get a raise last year. Wanda has worked on the assembly line at the GM plant since last year. So Wanda almost certainly got a raise.

Analysis   This is a strong argument.

In comparison, the following are usually too vague to reason with:

most	a few	a number of	many
a lot	mostly	quite a lot	a bunch of

But two vague generalities are clear enough for us to use well in our reasoning: ***almost all*** and ***a very few***.

Example 23   Almost all high school principals have an advanced degree. So the principal at Epstein High has an advanced degree.

Analysis   This is a strong argument. Compare it to the direct way of reasoning with "all."

Example 24   Almost all university professors teach every year. Mary Jane teaches every year. So Mary Jane is a university professor.

Analysis This is weak. Mary Jane could be a high school teacher. Compare it to arguing backwards with "all."

Example 25 Almost all dogs like ice cream. Almost all things that like ice cream don't bark. So almost all dogs don't bark.

    Analysis This is weak. Reasoning in a chain with "almost all" is just as weak as reasoning in a chain with "some."

Example 26 Very few army sergeants abused prisoners in Iraq. Janet is an army sergeant. So Janet did not abuse prisoners in Iraq.

    Analysis This is a strong argument. Compare it to the direct way of reasoning with "no."

Example 27 All truck drivers have a commercial driver's license. Only a very few beauticians have a commercial driver's license. So only a very few beauticians are truck drivers.

    Analysis This is strong. Compare it to the direct way of reasoning with "no."

Example 28 All professors get a paycheck at the end of the month. Only a very few people under 25 are professors. So only a very few people under 25 get a paycheck at the end of the month.

    Analysis This is weak. Compare it to arguing backwards with "no."

Here are some examples to help you learn how to determine whether an argument that uses general claims is valid or strong. For some you can refer to the forms above. But they all can be figured out if you return to the basics: It's not whether the premises and conclusion happen to be true, but rather, is there any possible way for the premises to be true and conclusion false, and if so, does it seem likely?

Example 29 Only managers can close out the cash register. George is a manager. So George can close out the cash register.

    Analysis This is weak. "Only" does not mean "all." George could be a manager in charge of the stock room.

Example 30 Everyone who wants to become a manager works hard. The people in Lois' group work hard. So the people in Lois' group want to become managers.

    Analysis This is weak. Maybe the workers in Lois' group

just want a raise and not the responsibility. The example illustrates a weak form: All S are Q; all P are Q; therefore, all S are P.

Example 31   No taxpayer who cheats is honest. Some dishonest people are found out. So some taxpayers who cheat are found out.
    Analysis   This is invalid and weak. It could be that the only people who are found out are ones who steal.

Example 32   All lions are fierce, but some lions are afraid of dogs. So some dogs aren't afraid of lions.
    Analysis   This is weak. Maybe the dogs don't recognize that the lions are afraid of them.

Example 33   Some nursing students aren't good at math. John is a nursing student. So John isn't good at math.
    Analysis   This is weak. John could be one of the many nursing students who is good at math.

Example 34   Every dog loves its master. Dick has a dog. So Dick is loved.
    Analysis   This is valid, but none of the forms we've studied show that.

Example 35   Almost every dog loves its master. Dick has a dog. So Dick is loved.
    Analysis   This is a strong and good argument.

Example 36   No one who reads this book is going to beg in the street. Because only poor people beg. And people who read this book won't be poor because they understand how to reason well.
    Analysis   This is a great argument. Trust us.

3.3 Prescriptive Claims

When we reason, we often want to conclude not only what is, but what ought to be.

> ***Descriptive and prescriptive claims*** A claim is descriptive if it says what is. A claim is prescriptive if it says what should be.

Every claim is either descriptive or prescriptive. Prescriptive claims are sometimes called *normative*, and descriptive claims are sometimes called *positive*.

Example 1 Drunken drivers kill more people than sober drivers.
    Analysis This is a descriptive claim.

Example 2 There should be a law against drunk driving.
    Analysis This is a prescriptive claim.

Example 3 Dick: I am hot.
Zoe: You should take your sweater off.
    Analysis Dick has made a descriptive claim. Zoe responds with a prescriptive claim.

Example 4 The government must not legalize marijuana.
    Analysis This is a prescriptive claim, using "must" to indicate "should."

Example 5 The government ought to lower interest rates.
    Analysis This is a prescriptive claim.

The words "good," "better," "best" and "bad," "worse," and "worst" and other ***value judgments*** are prescriptive when they carry with them the unstated assumption: "If it's good (preferable, . . .), then we (you) should do it; if it's bad, we (you) should not do it."

Example 6 Drinking and driving is bad.
Analysis This is prescriptive, carrying with it the assumption that we should not do what is bad.

A prescriptive claim either asserts a standard—this is what should be, and there's nothing more fundamental to say than that—or else it assumes another prescriptive claim as standard.

Example 7 Omar: Eating dogs is bad.
Analysis This is a prescriptive claim, since it carries with it the assumption that we should not eat dogs.

Zoe agreed with Omar when he said this to her. But did she really know what standard Omar had in mind? Certainly Omar's claim by itself is not the standard, but depends on something more fundamental. Perhaps he's a vegetarian and believes "You should treat all animals humanely, and butchering animals is not humane." In that case he almost certainly thinks the standard is objective. Zoe is likely to disagree, since she really enjoys eating a steak.

Or Omar might believe simply "Dogs taste bad." Then he has a subjective standard, which requires a further prescriptive one, "You shouldn't eat anything that tastes bad."

Or perhaps Omar believes "Dogs are carnivores, and we shouldn't eat carnivores." That would be a standard which he might support with what he considers a more basic standard, "We should not eat anything forbidden by the standard interpretation of the Koran, and the Koran forbids eating carnivores."

Or perhaps Omar just agrees with what most Americans think, "Dogs should be treated as companions to people and not as food." Then he would have an intersubjective standard.

Example 8 It's wrong to murder people.
Analysis This is a prescriptive claim. It's usually taken as a standard, rather than assuming another standard.

Example 9 The government ought to lower interest rates.
Analysis This is a prescriptive claim. Zoe's mother disagrees with Harry, since she wants to see her savings account earn more interest. Harry says the standard he is assuming is "The government should help the economy grow," which is what

he and Zoe's mom should debate.

When Dick hears this, he says that he agrees with Harry's standard, but he thinks that higher interest rates would make the economy grow.

Debates about prescriptive claims, then, should be about either the standard assumed or whether the claim follows from the standard. We cannot deduce a prescriptive claim from only descriptive claims, for a standard of values is needed first.

"Is" does not imply "ought" A prescriptive claim cannot be derived from premises all of which are descriptive.

Example 10 Smoking destroys people's health. So we ought to raise the tax on cigarettes.

Analysis The premise, a descriptive claim, is true, as we discuss in Section 4.6. But the conclusion does not follow without some prescriptive premise such as "We should tax activities that are destructive of people's health." Why we should believe that is then the issue.

Example 11 Epstein High should require students to wear uniforms in order to minimize gang signs.

Analysis This is really two prescriptive claims: "Epstein High should require students to wear uniforms" and then a reason why, "We should minimize gang signs (in school)."

Example 12 The government should raise the tax rate for the upper 1% of all taxpayers.

Analysis This is a prescriptive claim. Before we can judge whether to accept it, we need to know what standard lies behind that "should"—what does the speaker consider a good method of taxation?

Example 13 Tom: Capitalism is good because it raises the average income of everyone.

Analysis This is a prescriptive claim: "good" here has to be understood as implying that the system should be adopted. Tom might say that by "good economic system" he just means one that raises the average income of everyone in the society, but that would be a persuasive definition: the issue is whether that's what we think a good economic system should be.

Example 14 I totally don't support prohibiting smoking in bars—most people who go to bars do smoke and people should be aware that a bar is a place where a lot of people go to have a drink and smoke. There are no youth working or attending bars and I just don't believe you can allow people to go have a beer but not to allow people to have a cigarette—that's a person's God-given right.   Gordy Hicks, City Councilor, Socorro, N. M.
reported in *El Defensor Chieftain*, July 24, 2002

     Analysis The implicit standard here for why smoking shouldn't be prohibited in bars seems to be that society should not establish sanctions against any activity that doesn't corrupt youth or create harm to others who can't avoid it. The argument is just as good without the appeal to God, so by the Guide to repairing arguments we can ignore that. If it turns out that Hicks really does think the standard is theological, then the argument he gave isn't adequate.

     People who believe that all prescriptive claims are subjective are called *relativists*. They think that all standards—for beauty, morality, and every other value—are relative to what some person or group of people believe. Most people, though, believe that at least some prescriptive claims are objective, such as "You shouldn't torture people."
     Often when you challenge someone to make his or her standard explicit, they'll say, "I just mean it's wrong (right) to me." Yet when you press them, it turns out they're not so happy you disagree. They're being defensive, and what they really mean is "I have a right to believe that." Of course they do. But do they have a good reason to believe the claim? It's rare that people intend moral views to be taken as subjective.

4 Reasoning about Experience

In reasoning about our experience we draw comparisons, we use numbers and graphs, we generalize, we try to determine cause and effect. These kinds of reasoning require special skills. And there are particular problems with these kinds of reasoning that we should avoid.

In Section 4.1 we look at how to reason using comparisons. Analogies are typically incomplete arguments, but investigating them carefully can lead us to clarify our thinking.

In Section 4.2 we look at how numbers can be misused in making claims, and in Section 4.3 we look at how we can be misled by graphs.

Section 4.4 is about how we can generalize from our experience, arriving at true claims about a group from knowing something about only a part of that group. We'll see how to avoid lots of mistakes in generalizing.

Section 4.5 is devoted to the main concern of much of our lives: cause and effect. We'll see how to determine causes and how to avoid errors in reasoning about them. That will lead us in Section 4.6 to methods for determining causes from statistical evidence.

4.1 Analogies

> **Analogy** A comparison becomes reasoning by analogy when it is part of an argument: On one side of the comparison we draw a conclusion, so on the other side we say that we should conclude the same.

Example 1 We should legalize marijuana. After all, if we don't, what's the rationale for making alcohol and tobacco legal?
Analysis Alcohol is legal. Tobacco is legal. Therefore, marijuana should be legal. They are sufficiently similar. This is reasoning by analogy.

Example 2 DDT has been shown to cause cancer in rats. So there is a good chance DDT will cause cancer in humans.
Analysis This is reasoning by analogy: Rats are like humans. So if rats get cancer from DDT, so will humans.

Example 3 My love is like a red, red rose.
Analysis This is not reasoning by analogy: there's no argument.

An analogy is typically an incomplete argument that relies on an unstated general principle. The value of the analogy is often to uncover that principle.

Example 4 "Blaming soldiers for war is like blaming firemen for fires."

(Background: Country Joe MacDonald was a rock star who wrote songs protesting the war in Vietnam. In 1995 he was interviewed on National Public Radio about his motives for working to establish a memorial for Vietnam War soldiers in Berkeley, California, his home and a center of anti-war protests in the '60s and '70s. This claim was his response.)

Analysis   This is a comparison. But it's meant as an argument:

> We don't blame firemen for fires.
> Firemen and fires are like soldiers and wars.
> Therefore, we should not blame soldiers for war.

In what way are firemen and fires like soldiers and wars? They have to be similar enough in some respect for Country Joe's remark to be more than suggestive. We need to pick out important similarities that we can use as premises.

> *Firemen and fires are like soldiers and war.*
> wear uniforms
> answer to chain of command
> cannot disobey superior without serious consequences
> fight (fires/wars)
> work done when fire/war is over
> until recently only men
> lives at risk in work
> fire/war kills others
> firemen don't start fires—soldiers don't start wars
> usually like beer

That's stupid: Firemen and soldiers usually like beer. So?

When you ask "So?" you're on the way to deciding if the analogy is good. It's not just any similarity that's important. There must be some crucial, important way that firemen fighting fires is like soldiers fighting wars, some similarity that can account for why we don't blame firemen for fires that also applies to soldiers and war. Some of the similarities listed don't seem to matter. Others we can't use because they trade on an ambiguity, like saying firemen "fight" fires.

We don't have any good guide for how to proceed—that's a weakness of the original argument. But if we are to take Country Joe MacDonald's remark seriously, we have to come up with some principle that applies to both sides.

The similarities that seem most important are that both firemen and soldiers are involved in dangerous work, trying to end a problem/disaster they didn't start. We don't want to blame someone for helping to end a disaster that could harm us all.

(‡) Firemen are involved in dangerous work.
Soldiers are involved in dangerous work.
The job of a fireman is to end a fire.
The job of a soldier is to end a war.
Firemen don't start fires.
Soldiers don't start wars.

But even with these added to the original argument, we don't get a good argument for the conclusion that we shouldn't blame soldiers for wars. We need a general principle:

You shouldn't blame someone for helping to end a disaster that could harm others if he didn't start the disaster.

This general principle seems plausible, and it yields a valid argument.

But is the argument good? Are all the premises true? This is the point where the differences between firemen and soldiers might be important.

The first two premises of (‡) are clearly true, and so is the third. But is the job of soldiers to end a war? And do soldiers really not start wars? Look at this difference:

Without firemen there would still be fires.
Without soldiers there wouldn't be any wars.

Without soldiers there would still be violence. But without soldiers—any soldiers anywhere—there could be no organized violence of one country against another ("What if they gave a war and nobody came?" —an anti-war slogan of the Vietnam War era).

So? The analogy shouldn't convince. The argument has a dubious premise.

We did not prove that soldiers should be blamed for wars. As always, *when you show an argument is bad you haven't proved the conclusion false.* You've only shown that you have no more reason than before for believing the conclusion.

Perhaps the premises at (‡) could be modified, using that soldiers are drafted for wars. But that's beyond Country Joe's argument. If he meant something more, then it's his responsibility to flesh it out. Or we could use his comparison as a starting place to decide whether there is a general principle, based on the similarities, for why we shouldn't blame soldiers for war.

Evaluating an analogy

- Is this an argument? What is the conclusion?
- What is the comparison?
- What are the premises (the sides of the comparison)?
- What are the similarities?
- Can we state the similarities as premises and find a *general principle* that covers the two sides?
- Does the general principle really apply to both sides? Do the differences matter?
- Is the argument strong or valid? Is it good?

Example 5   It's wrong for the government to run a huge deficit—just as it's wrong for any family to overspend its budget.

Analysis   Here it is claimed that what is good for a person or family is also what is good for a country. Without more premises, though, this is unconvincing because of the enormous differences between a family and a country: a family doesn't have to repair roads, it can't put up tariffs, nor can it print money.

It's a *fallacy of composition* to argue that what is true of the individual is therefore true of the group, or what is true of the group is therefore true of the individual. The differences between them are typically too great for the analogy to be good.

Example 6   Tom: Homosexual marriage threatens the sanctity of marriage. We should outlaw it in order to protect children, since every child needs a mother and a father to raise it. A constitutional amendment is needed so the same laws hold throughout the U.S.

Zoe: The same argument could be made against divorce. So Britney Spears should still be married, because that one-day marriage she had was sure a slam against the "sanctity of marriage." And we should have a constitutional amendment outlawing divorce. And perhaps an amendment with severe penalties for out-of-wedlock births.

Analysis   Zoe is showing that Tom's argument is bad by showing that another argument "just like" his has a conclusion that we would consider absurd. Whatever general principle that makes his argument work must also apply in the other case. So Zoe has refuted Tom—though that doesn't mean his conclusion is false. *An analogy of one argument to another can be a powerful way to refute.* (Compare Examples 2 and 4 of Section 2.6 on killing flies.)

Analogies are at the heart of legal reasoning:

The basic pattern of legal reasoning is reasoning by example. It is reasoning from case to case. It is a three-step process described by the doctrine of precedent in which a proposition descriptive of the first case is made into a rule of law and then applied to a next similar situation. The steps are these: similarity is seen between cases; next the rule of law inherent in the first case is announced; then the rule of law is made applicable to the second case.

Edward H. Levi, *An Introduction to Legal Reasoning*

Example 7 The Supreme Court has decided it is a constitutional right for a doctor to terminate medical treatment that prolongs the life of a terminally ill or brain-dead person, so long as the doctor acts according to the wishes of that person (*Cruzan vs. Director, Missouri Department of Health*, 497 U.S. 261). So the Supreme Court should decide that assisting someone to commit suicide, a person who is terminally ill or in great suffering, as Dr. Kevorkian did, is a constitutionally protected right (*Compassion in Dying vs. State of Washington*).

Analysis Are the two situations similar? The court should decide with respect to the actual incidents in these cases. The court can decide narrowly, by saying this new case is not sufficiently like *Cruzan*, or broadly, by enunciating a principle that applies in both cases or else distinguishes between them. Or it can bring in more cases for comparison in trying to decide what general principle applies. (You can look up on the Internet how the court decided.)

4.2 Numbers

Example 1 There were twice as many rapes as murders in our town.
    Analysis This seems to say something important, but what? It's a meaningless comparison, like comparing *apples and oranges*.

Example 2 It's getting really violent here. There were 8% more murders this year than last.
    Analysis This is a mistaken comparison. If the town is growing rapidly and the number of tourists is growing even faster, it would be no surprise that the *number* of murders is going up, though the *rate* (how many murders per 100,000 population) might be going down. It's safer to live in a town of one million with 20 murders last year than in a small town of 25,000 that had 6.

Often numbers are used to make a comparison look impressive. But such a comparison is worthless, just *two times zero is still zero*, if the base of the comparison is not stated.

Example 3 A clothing store advertises a sale of sweaters at "25% off." You take it to mean 25% off the price they used to charge which was $20, so you'd pay $15. But the store could mean 25% off the suggested retail price of $26, so it's now $19.50. You have to ask, "25% off *what?*"

Example 4 Tom sees a stock for $60 and thinks it's a good deal. He buys it; a week later it's at $90, so he sells. He made $30— a 50% gain! His friend Wanda hears about it and buys the stock at $90; a week later it goes down to $60, so she panics and sells the stock. Wanda lost $30—that's a $33 1/3% loss. The same $30 is a different percentage depending on where you started.

$$50\% \uparrow \begin{bmatrix} \$90 \\ \$60 \end{bmatrix} \downarrow 33^{1}/_{3}\%$$

Example 5   Heard on National Public Radio: "Breast feeding is up 16% from 1989."
   Analysis   Up 16% from what? Besides, how could they know? Who was looking in all those homes? A survey? Whom did they ask? Women chosen randomly? But lots of them don't have infants. Women who visited doctors? But lots of women, lots of poor ones, don't see a doctor. What does "breast feeding" mean? Does a woman who breast feeds one day and then gives it up qualify as someone who breast feeds? Or one who breast feeds two weeks? Six months? *Often numbers are cited where it is clear there is no way the number could be known.* Maybe NPR is reporting on a reliable survey, but without further information, we should treat it as just noise.

Mean, median, and mode
The *mean* or *average* of a collection of numbers is
   obtained by adding the numbers and then
   dividing by the number of items.
The *median* is the midway mark: the same number
   of items above as below.
The *mode* is the number most often attained.

The *average* of 7, 9, 37, 22, 109, 9, 11 is calculated:
   Add $7 + 9 + 37 + 22 + 109 + 9 + 11 = 204$
   Divide   204 by 7 = 29.14, the average
The *median* is 11.
The *mode* is 9.

An average is a useful figure to know only if there isn't too much variation in the figures.

Example 6   The average number of people in a household in Las Vegas is 2.1.
   Analysis   So? With the large number of single-person households there, the median would be more informative. Better still would be to know the actual distribution over all families.

Example 7   The average wage of concert pianists in the U.S. is less than the average wage of university professors.

Analysis So? There's little variation in the salaries of university professors (almost all between $30,000 and $75,000), but there's a huge variation in concert pianists' income ($15,000 vs. $2,000,000). The mode would be more informative.

Example 8 Dr. E's final exam

score	number of students
95	3 students
94	7 students
92	1 student
90	4 students
75	1 student
62	4 students
57	5 students
55	4 students
52	2 students

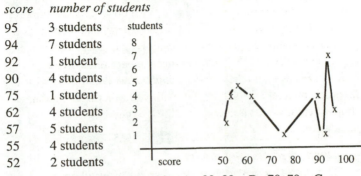

The grading scale was 90–100 = A, 80–89 = B, 70–79 = C, 60–69 = D, 59 and below = F. When Dr. E's department head asked her how the teaching went, he told her, "Great, just like you wanted, the average mark was 75%, a C." But she knows Dr. E too well to be satisfied. She asks him, "What was the median score?" Again Dr. E can reply, "75." As many got above 75 as below 75. But knowing how clever Dr. E is with numbers, she asks him what the mode score was. Dr. E flushes, "Well, 94." Now she knows something is fishy. When she wanted the average score to be about 75, she was thinking of a graph that looked like:

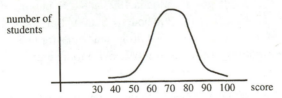

The distribution of the marks should be in a bell-shape: clustered around the median.

Unless you have good reason to believe that the average is pretty close to the median and that the distribution is more or less bell-shaped, the average isn't informative.

4.3 Graphs

Graphs can be useful in making comparisons. But they can conceal claims, mislead, or just be wrong.

Example 1

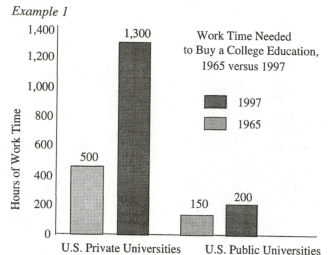

W. J. Baumol and A. S. Blinder, *Economics*

Analysis This graph from an economics textbook looks clear, but personal experience should tell you it's wrong. The authors say the average hourly wage is about $13. So according to the graph the (average?) cost of a college education in 1997 at a U.S. public university was about $13/hour x 200 hours = $2600. But that wouldn't have been enough for even tuition and books for one year, much less housing and board—let alone for four years.

Example 2

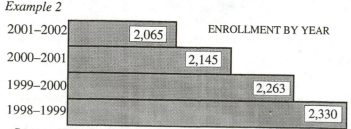

Socorro, N.M. Consolidated Schools Accountability Report, 2000–2001

Analysis The numbers here are correct, but the graph
greatly exaggerates the differences between years. The enrollment
in 2001– 2002 is 11.4% less than in 1998–1999, but the difference
in the lengths of the bars representing those enrollments is 66%.
Visually the difference appears even greater because we're
comparing areas instead of comparing lengths.

Example 3

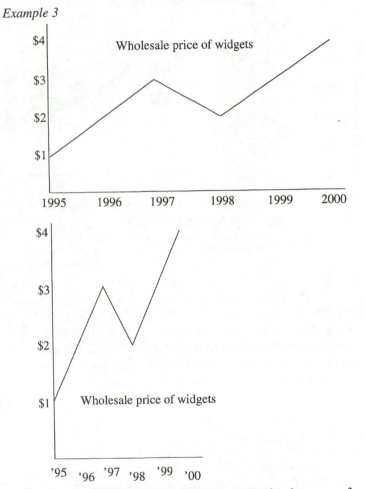

Analysis Here you can see how the angle, the sharpness of
increase and decrease, can be exaggerated greatly by the spacing of
the scales on the axes. This affects our perception of the volatility

and the amount of increase or decrease of prices. *Graphs can create misleading comparisons by the choice of how the measuring points on the axes are spaced.*

Example 4   An economics text gives this graph and remarks that from 1966 to 1982 the prices of stocks were generally going down.

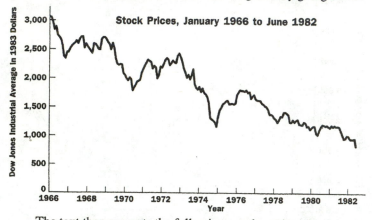

The text then presents the following graph, noting that from 1993 to 1998 stock prices were generally going up.

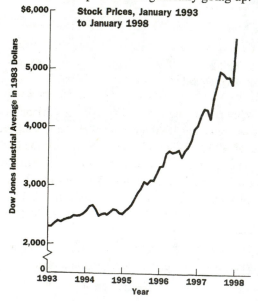

The text then gives a fuller graph.

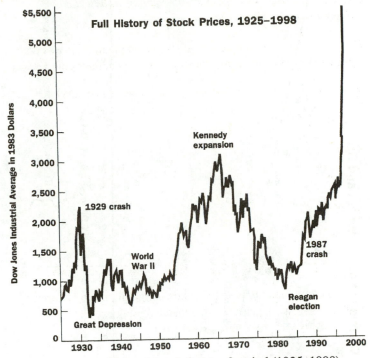

Full History of Stock Prices, 1925–1998

"A much longer and less-biased choice of period (1925–1998)
gives a less distorted picture. It indicates that investments in stocks
are sometimes profitable and sometimes unprofitable."

W. J. Baumol and A. S. Blinder, *Economics*

Analysis Why is the longer period apt for comparison to the
present day? If we looked at 1890 onwards, we'd have a different
picture still (the label "Full History" is wrong). Maybe the best
comparison for an analogy about investing in stocks is with the
later periods because of new regulations on buying and selling
stocks. The graphs do, however, compensate for inflation by
stating the values in 1983 dollars. If they didn't, it would be just
apples and oranges.

Also note how the steepness of the increases and decreases
are exaggerated in this last graph compared to the others.

Example 5

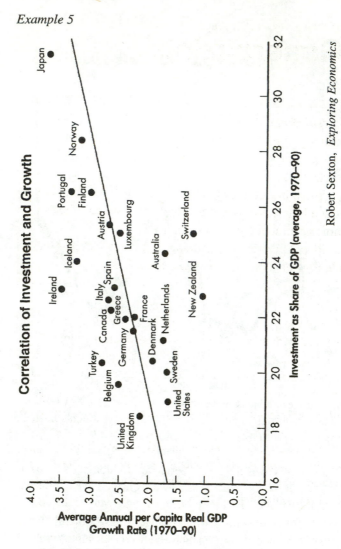

Robert Sexton, Exploring Economics

Analysis By drawing the line in this graph, the author is asserting that investment and growth are correlated: both rise together. His premises are the data plotted as points. But the picture doesn't obviously support that. Why draw a line rather than a curve? And why this line? We can accept the correlation on the basis of this graph only if we take it as an appeal to the author's authority.

4.4 Generalizing

> *Generalizing* To generalize is to conclude a claim about a group, the *population*, from a claim about some part of it, the *sample*. To generalize is to make an argument.
>
> Sometimes the general claim that is the conclusion is called the *generalization*; sometimes we call the whole argument a generalization.
>
> Plausible premises about the sample are called the *inductive evidence* for the generalization.

Example 1 In a study of 5,000 people who owned pets in Anchorage, Alaska, dog owners expressed higher satisfaction with their pets and with their own lives. So dog owners are more satisfied with their pets and their own lives than other pet owners.

Analysis Sample: The 5,000 people who were surveyed in Anchorage. *Population*: Pet owners everywhere.

Example 2 Of potential customers surveyed, 72% said that they liked "very much" the new green color that Yoda plans to use for its cars. So about 72% of all potential customers will like it.

Analysis Sample: The group of potential customers interviewed. *Population*: All potential customers. This is a statistical generalization.

Example 3 Every time the minimum wage is raised, there's squawking that it will cause inflation and decrease employment. And every time it doesn't. So watch for the same bad arguments again this time.

Analysis The unstated conclusion is that raising the minimum wage will not cause inflation or decrease employment. This is a generalization from the past to the future.
Sample: All times in the past that the minimum wage has risen.
Population: All times it has risen or will rise.

Example 4   The doctor tells you to fast from 10 p.m. At 10 a.m. she gives you glucose to drink. Forty-five minutes later she takes some of your blood and has it analyzed. She concludes you don't have diabetes.

   Analysis   Sample: The blood the doctor took. *Population*: All the blood you have in your body.

Example 5   Wanda goes to the city council meeting with a petition signed by all the people who live on her block requesting that a street light be put in. Addressing the city council, she says, "Everyone on this block wants a street light here."

   Analysis   This is not a generalization. There's no argument from some to more, since the sample equals the population.

What constitutes a good generalization? Consider first the sample.

Representative sample   A sample in which no one subgroup of the whole population is represented more than its proportion in the population.

   A sample is *biased* if it is not representative.

For a generalization to be good we should have a representative sample. But how can we get one? You might think we can get one by *haphazard sampling*: choosing with no intentional bias. But that's not reliable.

Example 6   To determine the attitudes of students about sex before marriage, Tom gave a questionnaire to the first 20 students he met coming out of the student union. He was choosing his sample haphazardly. That sample may be representative, but there's no reason to believe so. Those students might be coming from a meeting of the Green Party, or the student Bible Society, or .... . Advised of the problem, Tom enlisted three of his friends to give the questionnaire to the first 20 students they meet coming out of the student union, the administration offices, and the largest classroom building at 9 a.m., 1 p.m., and 6 p.m. But there's no reason to think that new sample is representative either—all the players on intercollegiate sports teams might be gone for the day.

> **Random sampling**   A sample is chosen randomly
> if at every choice there is an equal chance for any of
> the remaining members of the population to be picked.

Example 7   So Tom thinks to assign a number to each student, write the numbers on slips of paper, put them in a fishbowl, and draw one number at a time. That probably would be a random selection. But there's a chance that slips with longer numbers will have more ink and fall to the bottom of the bowl when you shake it. Or the slips aren't all the same size. So usually to get a random selection we use prepared tables of random numbers, which can be made even by a spreadsheet program for a home computer. For Tom's survey he could get a list of all students; if the first number on the table is 413 he'd pick the 413th student on the list; if the second number is 711, he'd pick the 711th student on the list; and so on, until he has a sample that's big enough.

Random sampling is very likely going to yield a sample that is representative. That's because of the *law of large numbers*, which says, roughly, that if the probability of something occurring is X percent, then over the long run the percentage of times that happens will be about X percent.

Example 8   The probability of a flip of a fair coin landing heads is 50%. So though you may get a run of 8 tails, then 5 heads, then 4 tails, then 36 heads to start, in the long run, repeating the flipping, eventually the number of heads will tend toward 50%.

Example 9   Suppose that of the 20,000 students at your school, 500 are gay males. Then the chance that *one* student picked at random would be a gay male is: 500/20,000 = 1/40. If Tom were to pick 300 students at random, the chance that half of them would be gay is very, very small. It is very likely, however, that 7 or 8 (1/40 of 300) will be gay males.

Example 10   Dick (at a roulette table): It's come up red 12 times in a row. It's bound to come up black several times in a row now.
   Analysis   This is a bad application of the law of large numbers. The ball could land on red 100 times in a row, and black

could even out by coming up just 1 more time than red every 100 spins for the next 10,000 spins. The *gambler's fallacy* is to reason that a run of events of a certain kind makes a run of contrary events more likely to even up the probabilities.

If you choose a large sample randomly, the chance is very high that it will be representative. That's because the chance of any one subgroup being over-represented is small—not nonexistent, but small. It doesn't matter if you know anything about the composition of the population in advance. After all, to know how many homosexuals there are, and how many married women, and how many men, and . . . you'd need to know almost everything about the population in advance. But that's what you use surveys to find out.

With a random sample we have good reason to believe the sample is representative. A sample chosen haphazardly *might give* a representative sample—but we have no good reason to *believe* it will be representative.

Weak Argument	*Strong Argument*
Sample is chosen *haphazardly*. Therefore, the sample is representative.	Sample is chosen *randomly*. Therefore, the sample is representative.
Lots of ways the sample could be biased.	Very unlikely the sample is biased.

Example 11 The classic example that haphazard sampling can be bad, even with an enormous sample, is the poll done in 1936 by *Literary Digest.* The magazine mailed out 10,000,000 ballots asking who the person would vote for in the 1936 presidential election. They received 2,300,000 back. With that huge sample, the magazine confidently predicted that Alf Landon would win. Roosevelt received 60% of the vote, one of the biggest wins ever. What went wrong? The magazine selected its sample from lists of its own subscribers and telephone and automobile owners. In 1936 that was the wealthy class, which preferred Alf Landon.

Further, we need to know that the size of the sample is

big enough in order to rely on a generalization. But how big? Roughly, the idea is to measure how much more likely it is that your generalization is going to be accurate as you increase the number in your sample. If you want to find out how many people in your class of 300 economics students are spending 10 hours a week on the homework, you might ask 15 or 20. If you interview 30 you might get a better picture, but there's a limit. After you've asked 100, you probably won't get a much different result if you ask 150. And if you've asked 200, it's not likely that your generalization will be different if you ask 250.

Often you can rely on common sense when small numbers are involved. Generalizing from a sample that is obviously too small is called a *hasty generalization* based on *anecdotal evidence*. But when we generalize to a very large population, say 2,500, or 25,000, or 250,000,000, how big the sample should be cannot be explained without at least a mini-course on statistics. In evaluating statistical generalizations, you have to expect that the people doing the sampling have looked at enough examples, which is reasonable if it's a respected organization, a well-known polling company, physicians, or a drug company that has to answer to the Food and Drug Administration. Surprisingly, perhaps, 1500 is typically adequate for the sample size when surveying all adults in the U.S.

How big the sample needs to be also depends on how much *variation* there is in the population regarding the aspect you're investigating. If there is very little variation, then a small sample chosen haphazardly will do. Lots of variation (or in a case where you don't know how much variation there is) demands a very large sample, and random sampling is the best way to get a representative one.

Example 12 It's incredible how much information they can put on a CD. I just bought one that contains a whole encyclopedia.

Analysis This is a good generalization. The unstated conclusion is that every CD can contain as much information as this one that has the encyclopedia on it. There is little variation in the production of CDs for computers, so a sample of one is sufficient.

Finally, the sample has to be studied well.

Example 13   The doctor taking your blood to see if you have diabetes won't get a reliable result if her test tube isn't clean or if she forgets to tell you to fast the night before. You won't find out the real attitudes of students about tuition if you ask a biased question. Picking a random sample of bolts won't help you determine whether the bolts are O.K. if all you do is inspect them visually, not with a microscope or a stress test.

Example 14   Surveys on sexual habits are notorious for inaccurate reporting: Invariably the number of times that women in the U.S. report they engaged in sexual intercourse with a man in the last week, or month, or year, is much lower than the reports that men give of sexual intercourse with a woman during that time. The figures are so different that it would be impossible for both groups to be answering accurately. Generally, questionnaires and surveys are problematic, because questions need to be formulated without bias. Even then, the interviewer has to rely on the respondents answering truthfully.

Premises needed for a good generalization
- The sample is representative.
- The sample is big enough.
- The sample is studied well.

Still, it's never reasonable to believe a statistical generalization whose conclusion is exactly precise.

Example 15   In a survey, 27% of the people in Socorro who were interviewed said they wear glasses, so 27% of all people in Socorro wear glasses.

   Analysis   No matter how many people in Socorro are surveyed, short of virtually all of them, we can't be confident that exactly 27% of all people in the town wear glasses. Rather, "27%, more or less, wear glasses" is the right conclusion.

That "more or less" can be made fairly precise according to a theory of statistics. The *margin of error* gives the range in which the actual number for that population is likely to fall. The *confidence level* measures how strong the argument is for the statistical conclusion, where the survey method and responses are taken as premises.

Example 16 The opinion poll says that when voters were asked their preference, the incumbent was favored by 53% and the challenger by 47%, with a margin of error of 2% and a confidence level of 95%. So the incumbent will win tomorrow.

Analysis From this survey they are concluding that the percentage of all voters who favor the incumbent is between 51% and 55%, while the challenger is favored by between 45% and 49%. "The confidence level is 95%" means that there is a 95% chance it's true that the actual percentage of voters who prefer the incumbent is between 51% and 55%. If the confidence level were 70%, then the survey wouldn't be reliable: There would be a 3-out-of-10 chance the conclusion is false. Typically, if the confidence level is below 95%, results won't be announced.

The bigger the sample, the higher the confidence level and the lower the margin of error. The problem always is to decide how much it's worth in extra time and expense to increase the sample size in order to get a stronger argument.

Example 17 With a shipment of 30 insulating tiles, inspecting 3 and finding them O.K. would normally allow you to conclude that all the tiles are O.K. But if they're for the space shuttle, where a bad tile could doom the spacecraft, you'd want to inspect each and every one of them.

Risk doesn't change how strong an argument we have, only how strong an argument we want before we'll accept the conclusion.

One common mistake in making generalizations is to pay *selective attention*: We note only what's unusual. It seems that buttered toast always lands buttered side down because we notice when it does.

Example 18 Every time I've seen a stranger at Dick's gate, Spot has barked. So Spot will always bark at strangers at Dick's gate.

    Analysis This is a bad generalization: The sample is chosen haphazardly, so there's no reason to believe it's representative.

Example 19 In a study of 5,000 people who owned pets in Anchorage, Alaska, dog owners expressed higher satisfaction with their pets and their lives. So dog owners are more satisfied with their pets and their own lives.

    Analysis This is a bad generalization. The sample is clearly not representative. At best the evidence could lead to a conclusion about all pet owners in Anchorage, Alaska.

Example 20 Maria asked all but three of the thirty-six people in her class whether they've ever used heroin. Only two said "yes." So Maria concludes that almost no one in the class has used heroin.

    Analysis This is a bad generalization. The sample is big enough and representative, but it's not studied well. People are not likely to admit to a stranger that they've used heroin; an anonymous questionnaire is needed.

Example 21 My grandmother was diagnosed with cancer seven years ago. She refused any treatment that was offered to her over the years. She's perfectly healthy and doing great. The treatment for cancer is just a scam to get people's money.

    Analysis This is a bad generalization. It's just anecdotal evidence.

Example 22 Dick: A study I read said people with large hands are better at math.

    Suzy: I guess that explains why I can't divide.

    Analysis This is a bad application of a generalization. Perhaps the study was done carefully with a random sample. But you don't need a study to know that people with large hands do better at math: Babies have small hands, and they can't even add. *All people* is the wrong population to study.

Example 23 "According to the National Pork Producers Council (www.nppc.org), average hog market weight is 250 pounds, and it takes about 3.5 pounds of feed to produce one pound of live hog weight."

Analysis It's a good appeal to authority to accept this generalization given by the National Pork Producers Council. Though we don't have access to the data they used nor how they interpreted it, they are a big enough organization to employ good statisticians, and they have no reason to lie to their own members.

Example 24 Lee: Every rich person I've met invested heavily in the stock market. So I'll invest in the stock market, too.

Analysis This is a confused attempt to generalize. Perhaps Lee thinks that the evidence he cites gives the conclusion that if you invest in the stock market, you'll get rich(er). But that's arguing backwards, confusing (1) "If you invest in the stock market, you'll get rich" with (2) "If you're rich, then you will have invested in the stock market." The population for (1) is all investors in the stock market, not just the rich ones. It's a case of selective attention.

Example 26 People in New Mexico are very independent and almost always prefer to live in separate homes rather than apartments. So we should allow for more subdivisions to be built in Albuquerque.

Analysis If we drop the vague phrase "are very independent," the premise here is a general claim that we shouldn't accept without a good generalization establishing it. The conclusion of the argument is a prescriptive claim that requires some prescriptive premise.

Example 27 Of chimpanzees fed one pound of chocolate per day in addition to their usual diet, 72% became obese within two months. Therefore, it is likely that most humans who eat 2% of their body weight in chocolate daily will become obese within two months.

Analysis A generalization is needed to make this analogy good: 72% of all chimpanzees, more or less, will become obese if fed one pound of chocolate per day in addition to their usual diet. Whether this is a good generalization will depend on whether the researchers can claim that their sample is representative. The analogy then needs a claim about the similarity of chimpanzee physiology to human physiology.

4.5 Cause and Effect

What exactly is a *cause*? Consider what Dick said last night:

Spot made me wake up.

Spot is the thing that somehow caused Dick to wake up. But it's not just that Spot existed. It's what he was doing that caused Dick to wake up:

Spot's barking caused Dick to wake up.

So Spot's barking is the cause? What kind of thing is that? The easiest way to describe the cause is to say:

Spot barked.

The easiest way to describe the effect is to say:

Dick woke up.

Causes and effects can be described with claims.

> **Causal claims** A causal claim is a claim that can be rewritten as "X causes (caused) Y."
>
> A *particular* causal claim is one in which a single claim can describe the (purported) cause and a single claim can describe the (purported) effect. A *general* causal claim is a causal claim that generalizes many particular causal claims.

For example, "Spot caused Dick to wake up" is a particular causal claim, where the purported cause can be described by the single claim "Spot was barking," and the purported effect by "Dick woke up." We could generalize from this particular cause and effect to, for example, "Very loud barking by someone's dog near him when he is sleeping *causes* him to wake, if he's not deaf." This is a general causal claim. For it to be true, lots of particular causal claims must be true.

Example 1 The police car's siren got Dick to pull over.

Analysis This is a particular causal claim. The purported cause can be described by "The police car had its siren going," and the purported effect by "Dick pulled over."

Example 2 The speeding ticket Dick got made his auto insurance rate go up.

Analysis This is a particular causal claim. The purported cause is "Dick got a speeding ticket," and the effect is "Dick's auto insurance went up."

Example 3 Speeding tickets make people's auto insurance rates go up.

Analysis This is a general causal claim. For it to be true all particular causal claims like the one in the previous example have to be true.

Example 4 Penicillin prevents serious infection.

Analysis What is the cause? The existence of penicillin? No, it's that penicillin is administered to people in certain amounts at certain stages of their infections. What's a "serious infection"? This is too vague to count as a causal claim.

Example 5 Lack of rain caused the crops to fail.

Analysis The purported cause here is "There was no rain," and the purported effect is "The crops failed." This example was true a few years ago in the Midwest. Causes need not be something active; almost any claim that describes the world could qualify as a cause.

What conditions are needed for a causal claim to be true?

1. The cause and effect both happened. That is, both the claims describing the cause and effect have to be true. We wouldn't say that Spot's barking caused Dick to wake up if either Dick didn't wake up or Spot didn't bark.

2. It's (nearly) impossible for the cause to happen and the effect not to happen. That is, it has to be (nearly) impossible for the claim describing the cause to be true and the claim describing the effect to be false. For example, it can't be just coincidence that Dick woke up when Spot barked.

That's just the relation of premises to conclusion in a valid or strong argument. Only here we're not trying to convince anyone that the conclusion is true: We know that Dick woke up. What we can carry over from our study of arguments is how to look for all the possibilities—all the ways the premises could be true and the conclusion false—to determine if there is cause and effect. And just as with arguments, we will often need to supply unstated premises to show that the effect follows from the cause.

Example 6   A lot has to be true for it to be impossible for "Spot barked" to be true and "Dick woke up" to be false:

Dick was sleeping soundly up to the time that Spot barked.
Spot barked at 3 a.m.
Spot was close to where Dick was sleeping. . . .

We could go on forever. But as with arguments, we state what we think is important and leave out the obvious. If someone challenged us, we could add "There was no earthquake at the time"—but we just assume that.

> **Normal conditions**   The obvious and plausible claims that are needed to establish that the relation between purported cause and purported effect is valid or strong are called the normal conditions for the causal claim.

For a general causal claim, such as "Very loud barking by someone's dog near him when he is sleeping *causes* him to wake, if he's not deaf," the normal conditions won't be specific just to the one time Spot woke Dick, but will be general.

3. The cause precedes the effect. The claims describing the cause become true before the claim describing the effect.

Example 7 We wouldn't accept that Spot's barking caused Dick to wake up if Spot began barking only after Dick woke up. The cause has to precede the effect. That is, "Spot barked" became true before "Dick woke up" became true. For there to be cause and effect, the cause has to become true before the effect becomes true.

4. The cause makes a difference. If there were no cause, there would be no effect.

Example 8 Dr. E has a desperate fear of elephants. So he buys a special wind chime and puts it outside his door to keep the elephants away. He lives in Cedar City, Utah, at 6,000 feet above sea level in a desert, and he confidently claims that the wind chime causes the elephants to stay away. After all, ever since he put up the wind chime he hasn't seen any elephants.

Why are we sure the wind chime being up did *not* cause elephants to stay away? Because even if there had been no wind chime, the elephants would have stayed away. Which elephants? All elephants. The wind chime works, but so would anything else. The wind chime doesn't make a difference. *Checking that the cause makes a difference is how we make sure we haven't overlooked another possible cause.*

5. There is no common cause. We don't say that night causes day, because there is a common cause of both "It was night" and "It is now day," namely, "The earth is rotating relative to the sun."

Example 9 Dick: Zoe is irritable because she can't sleep properly.

Tom: Maybe it's because she's been drinking so much espresso that she's irritable and can't sleep properly.

Analysis Tom hasn't shown that Dick's causal claim is false by raising the possibility of a common cause. But he does put

Dick's claim in doubt. We have to check the other conditions for cause and effect to see which causal claim seems most likely.

Necessary criteria for cause and effect

• The cause and effect happened (are true).

• It is (nearly) impossible for the cause to happen (be true) and the effect not to happen (be false), given the normal conditions.

• The cause precedes the effect.

• The cause makes a difference—if the cause had not happened, the effect would not have happened, given the normal conditions.

• There is no common cause.

Common mistakes in reasoning about cause and effect

A. *Tracing the cause too far back in time*   It's sometimes said that the cause must be close in space and time to the effect. But the astronomer is right when she says that a star shining caused the image on the photograph, even though that star is very far away, and the light took millions of years to arrive. The problem isn't how distant in time and space the cause is from the effect. The problem is how much has come between the cause and effect—whether we can specify the normal conditions. *When we trace a cause too far back, the problem is that the normal conditions begin to multiply.* There are too many conditions for us to imagine what would be necessary to establish that it is impossible for the cause to have been true and the effect false. When you get that far, you know you've gone too far.

Example 10   My mother missed the sign-up to get me into Kernberger Elementary School, and that's why I've never been able to get a good job.

   Analysis   This is tracing the cause too far back to be able to state the normal conditions.

B. *Reversing cause and effect* If reversing cause and effect sounds just as plausible as the original claim, investigate the evidence further before making a judgment.

Example 11 Suzy: Sitting too close to the TV ruins your eyesight.
Zoe: How do you know?
Suzy: Well, four of my grade school friends used to sit really close to the TV, and all of them wear really thick glasses now.
Zoe: Maybe they sat so close because they had bad eyesight.
Analysis Zoe hasn't shown that Suzy's claim is false. But her suggestion that cause and effect are reversed raises sufficient doubt not to accept Suzy's claim without more evidence.

C. *Looking too hard for a cause* We look for causes because we want to understand, so we can control our future. But sometimes the best we can say is that it's *coincidence*.

Example 12 Before your jaw drops open in amazement when a friend tells you a piano fell on his teacher the day after your friend dreamt that he saw him in a recital, remember the law of large numbers: If it's possible, given long enough, it'll happen. After all, most of us dream—say one dream a night for fifty million adults in the U.S. That's three hundred and fifty million dreams per week. With the elasticity in interpreting dreams and what constitutes a "dream coming true," it would be amazing if a lot of dreams *didn't* "accurately predict the future."

But doesn't everything have a cause? Shouldn't we look for it? For much that happens in our lives we won't be able to figure out the cause—we just don't know enough. We must, normally, ascribe lots of happenings to chance, to coincidence, or else we have paranoia and end up paying a lot of money to phone psychics.

D. *Post hoc ergo propter hoc* ("after this, therefore because of this") It's a mistake to argue that there is cause and effect just because one claim became true after another.

Example 13 I scored well on that last exam and I was wearing my red striped shirt. I'd better wear it every time I take an exam.
Analysis This is just *post hoc* reasoning.

Example 14   A recent study showed that everyone who uses heroin started with marijuana. So smoking marijuana causes heroin use.

Analysis   And they all probably drank milk first, too. Without further evidence this is just *post hoc* reasoning.

The best way to avoid making common mistakes in reasoning about cause and effect is to *experiment*. Conjecture possible causes, then by experiment eliminate them until there is only one. Check that one: Does it make a difference? If the purported cause is eliminated, is there still the effect? Often we can't do an experiment, but we can do an imaginary experiment. That's what we've always done in checking for validity: *Imagine the possibilities*.

Here is an example that shows all the steps in evaluating a causal claim.

Example 15

The cat made Spot run away.

Cause   What is the cause? It's not just that a cat existed. Perhaps the cause is "A cat meowed close to Spot."

Effect   Spot ran away.

Cause and effect true   The effect is clearly true. The cause is highly plausible: Almost all things that meow (where people are walking dogs) are cats.

Cause precedes effect   Yes.

It is (nearly) impossible for the cause to be true and effect false   What needs to be assumed as "normal" here? Spot is on a walk with Dick. Dick is holding the leash loosely enough for Spot to get away. Spot chases cats. Spot heard the cat meow. We could go on, but this seems enough to guarantee that it's unlikely that the cat could meow near Spot and Spot not chase it.

The cause makes a difference Would Spot have run away even if the cat had not meowed near him? Apparently not, given those normal conditions, since Dick seems surprised that he ran off. But perhaps he would have even if he hadn't heard the cat, if he'd seen it. But that apparently wasn't the case. So let's revise the cause to: "Spot wasn't aware a cat was near him, and the cat meowed close to Spot, and Spot heard it." Now we can reasonably believe that the cause made a difference.

Is there a common cause? Perhaps the cat was hit by a meat truck and lots of meat fell out, and Spot ran away for that? No, Spot wouldn't have barked. Nor would he have growled.

Perhaps the cat is a hapless bystander in a fight between dogs, one of whom is Spot's friend. We do not know if this is the case. So it's possible that there's a common cause, but it seems unlikely.

Evaluation: We have good reason to believe the original claim on the revised interpretation that the cause is "Spot wasn't aware a cat was near him, the cat meowed close to Spot, and Spot heard it."

These are the steps we should go through in establishing a causal claim. But if we can show that one of them fails, there's no need to check all the others.

Example 16 The President's speech on farm issues made the price of corn rise 17% the next day.

Analysis The purported cause is "The President gave a speech on farm issues," and the purported effect is "The price of corn rose 17% the next day." Did the purported cause make a difference? A few hours after the President's speech, crop reports were released that showed the corn harvest would be down 13% due to drought. Those reports alone would have been enough to ensure higher corn prices. We have no reason to believe that the President's speech was the cause.

Example 17 Money causes counterfeiting.

Analysis This is a general causal claim covering every

particular claim like "That there was money in this society caused this person to counterfeit the currency." We certainly have lots of inductive evidence. The problem seems to be that, though this is true, it's uninteresting. It's tracing the cause too far back. There being money in a society is part of the normal conditions when we have the effect that someone counterfeited currency.

Example 18 When more and more people are thrown out of work, unemployment results. President Calvin Coolidge
   Analysis This isn't cause and effect; it's a definition.

Example 19 God caused the universe.
   Analysis This is not a causal claim. It's just an odd way of saying "God created the universe."

Example 20 Maria: Fear of getting fired causes me to get to work on time.
   Analysis What is fear? The purported cause here is "Maria is afraid of getting fired," the effect: "Maria gets to work on time."
   Is it possible for Maria to be afraid of getting fired and still not get to work on time? Certainly, but not, perhaps, under normal conditions: Maria sets her alarm; the electricity doesn't go off; there isn't bad weather; Maria doesn't oversleep; . . .
   But doesn't the causal claim mean it's because she's afraid that Maria makes sure that these claims will be true, or that she'll get to work even if one or more is false? She doesn't let herself oversleep due to her fear. In that case how can we judge whether what Maria said is true? It's easy to think of cases where the cause is true and effect false. So we have to add normal conditions. But that Maria gets to work regardless of conditions that aren't normal is what makes her consider her fear to be the cause.
   Subjective causes are often a matter of feeling, some sense that we control what we do. They are often too vague for us to classify as true or false.

Example 21 Tom: The only time I've had a really bad backache is right after I went bicycling early in the morning when it was so cold last week. Bicycling never bothered me before. So it must be the cold weather that caused my back to hurt after cycling.
   Analysis The purported cause: "It was cold when Tom went cycling," the effect: "Tom got a backache." The criteria seem to be

satisfied. But Tom may have overlooked another cause. He also had an upset stomach, so maybe it was the flu. Or maybe it was tension, since he'd had a fight with Suzy the night before. He'll have to try cycling in the cold again to find out. Even then he may be looking too hard for *the* cause, when there may be several causes jointly. Another possibility: Tom will never know for sure.

Example 22 My neighbor said it's been the worst season ever for allergies this spring, but I told her I hadn't had any bad days. Then today I started sneezing. Darn it—if only she hadn't told me.

Analysis This may be cause and effect, but the evidence shouldn't convince. It's just *post hoc ergo propter hoc.*

Example 23 The Treaty of Versailles caused World War II.

Analysis The purported cause is "The Treaty of Versailles was agreed to and enforced." The purported effect is "World War II occurred." To analyze a conjecture like this an historian will write a book. The normal conditions have to be spelled out. He has to show that it was a foreseeable consequence of the enforcement of the Treaty of Versailles that Germany would re-arm. But was it foreseeable that Chamberlain would back down over Czechoslovakia? More plausible is that the signing of the Treaty of Versailles is *a* cause, not *the* cause of World War II. When several claims together are taken jointly as the cause, we say that each describes *a cause* or is a *causal factor*.

Example 24 Dick: Hold the steering wheel.
Zoe: What are you doing? Stop! Are you crazy?
Dick: I'm just taking my sweater off.
Zoe: I can't believe you did that. It's *so* dangerous.
Dick: Don't be silly. I've done it a thousand times before.
   Crash . . . Later
Dick: You had to turn the steering wheel!? That made us crash.

Analysis The purported cause is that Zoe turned the steering wheel. The effect is that the car crashed. The necessary criteria are satisfied. But as they say in court, Zoe's turning the steering wheel is a *foreseeable consequence* of Dick making her take the wheel, which is the real cause. The normal conditions are not just what has to be true before the cause, but also what will normally *follow* the cause.

Example 23 Dick: Wasn't that awful what happened to old Mr. Grzegorczyk?

Zoe: You mean those tree trimmers who dropped a huge branch on him and killed him?

Dick: You only got half the story. He'd had a heart attack in his car and pulled over to the side. He was lying on the pavement when the branch hit him and would have died anyway.

Analysis What's the cause of death? Mr. Grzegorczyk would have died anyway. So the tree branch falling on him wouldn't have made a difference.

But the tree branch falling on him isn't a foreseeable consequence, part of the normal conditions of his stumbling out of his car with a heart attack. It's an *intervening cause*.

Example 24 Poltergeists are making the pictures fall down from their hooks.

Analysis To accept this, we have to believe that poltergeists exist. That's dubious. Worse, it's probably not *testable*: How could you determine if there are poltergeists? Dubious claims that aren't testable are the worst candidates for causes.

Example 25 Running over nails causes your tires to go flat.

Analysis This is a plausible general causal claim. But it's wrong. There's not good inductive evidence. Lots of times we run over nails and our tires don't go flat. But sometimes they do. What's correct is: "Running over nails *can cause* your tires to go flat." That is, if the conditions are right, running over a nail will cause your tire to go flat.

The difference between "causes" and "can cause" is a difference between the normal conditions. For "causes" we feel we don't need much that isn't obvious; for "can cause" we feel that we could list claims, but they aren't perhaps "normal" ones we daily expect. We'll look at this in the next section.

4.6 Cause in Populations

When we say "Smoking causes lung cancer," what do we mean? If you smoke a cigarette you'll get cancer? If you smoke a lot of cigarettes this week, you'll get cancer? If you smoke 20 cigarettes a day for 40 years you'll get cancer? It can't be any of these, since we know smokers who did all that yet didn't get lung cancer, and the effect has to (almost) invariably follow the cause.

Cause in a population is usually explained as meaning that given the cause, there's a higher probability that the effect will be true than if there were not the cause. In this example, people who smoke have a much higher probability of getting lung cancer. But really we are talking about cause and effect just as we did before. Smoking lots of cigarettes over a long period of time will cause (inevitably) lung cancer. The problem is that we can't state, we have no idea how to state, nor is it likely that we'll ever be able to state the normal conditions for smoking to cause cancer. Among other factors, there is diet, where one lives, exposure to pollution and other carcinogens, and one's genetic inheritance. But *if we knew exactly* we'd say: "Under the conditions _____ , smoking ___ (number of) cigarettes every day for ___ years will result in lung cancer."

Since we can't specify the normal conditions, the best we can do is point to the evidence that convinces us that smoking is a cause of lung cancer and get an argument with a statistical conclusion: "People who continue to smoke two packs of cigarettes per day for ten years are ___% more likely (with margin of error of ___ %) to get lung cancer."

How do we establish cause in a population?

Controlled experiment: cause-to-effect This is our best evidence. We choose 10,000 people at random and ask 5,000 of them never to smoke and 5,000 of them to smoke a pack of cigarettes every day. We have two samples, one composed of those who are administered the cause, and one of those who are not, the latter called the *control group*. We come back 20 years later to check how many in each group got lung cancer. If a lot more of the smokers got lung cancer, and the groups were representative of the population as a whole, and we can see no other *common thread* among those who got lung cancer, we'd be justified in saying that smoking causes lung cancer. (Of course such an experiment would be unethical, so we use animals instead and then argue by analogy.)

Uncontrolled experiment: cause-to-effect   Here we take two randomly chosen, representative samples of the general population for which we have factored out other possible causes of lung cancer, such as working in coal mines. One of the groups is composed of people who say they never smoke. One group is composed of people who say they smoke. We follow the groups and 15–20 years later check whether those who smoked got lung cancer more often. Since we think we've accounted for other common threads, smoking is the remaining common thread that may account for why the second group got cancer more often.

     This is a *cause-to-effect* experiment, since we start with the suspected cause and see if the effect follows. But it is uncontrolled: Some people may stop smoking, some may begin, people may have quite variable diets—there may be a lot we'll have to factor out in trying to assess whether it's smoking that causes the extra cases of lung cancer.

Uncontrolled experiment: effect-to-cause   Here we look at as many people as possible who have lung cancer to see if there is some common thread that occurs in (almost all) their lives. We factor out those who worked in coal mines, we factor out those who lived in high pollution areas, those who drank a lot . . . . If it turns out that a much higher proportion of the remaining people smoked than in the general population, we have good evidence that smoking was the cause (the evaluation of this requires a knowledge of statistics). This is uncontrolled because how they got to the effect was unplanned, not within our control. And it is an *effect-to-cause* experiment because we start with the effect in the population and try to account for how it got there.

Example 1 Barbara smoked two packs of cigarettes each day for thirty years. Barbara now has lung cancer. Barbara's smoking caused her lung cancer.

Analysis Is it possible for Barbara to have smoked two packs of cigarettes each day for thirty years and not get lung cancer? We can't state the normal conditions. So we invoke the statistical relation between smoking and lung cancer to say it is unlikely for the cause to be true and effect false.

Does the cause make a difference? Could Barbara have gotten lung cancer even if she had not smoked? Suppose we know that Barbara wasn't a coal miner, didn't work in a textile factory, and didn't live in a city with a very polluted atmosphere, all conditions that are associated with a higher probability of getting lung cancer. Then it is possible for Barbara to have gotten lung cancer anyway, since some people who have no other risks do get lung cancer. But it is very unlikely, since very few of those people do.

We have no reason to believe that there is a common cause. It may be that people with a certain biological make-up feel compelled to smoke, and that biological make-up also contributes to their getting lung cancer independently of their smoking. But we have no evidence of such a biological factor.

So assuming a few normal conditions, "Barbara's smoking caused her lung cancer" is as plausible as the strength of the statistical link between smoking and lung cancer, and the strength of the link between not smoking and not getting lung cancer. We must be careful, though, that we do not attribute the cause of the lung cancer to smoking just because we haven't thought of any other cause, especially if the statistical link isn't very strong.

Example 2 Zoe: I can't understand Melinda. She's pregnant and she's drinking.

Dick: That's all baloney. I asked my mom, and she said she drank when she was pregnant with me. And I turned out fine.

Zoe: But think how much better you'd have been if she hadn't.

Analysis Zoe doesn't say but alludes to the cause-in-population claim that drinking during pregnancy causes birth defects or poor development of the child. That has been demonstrated: Many cause-in-population studies have been done that show there is a higher incidence of birth defects and developmental problems in children born to mothers who drink than to mothers who do not drink, and those defects and problems do not appear to arise from any other common factor.

Dick, however, makes a mistake. He confuses a cause-in-population claim with a general causal claim. He is right that his mother's experience would disprove the general causal claim, but it has no force against the cause-in-population claim.

Zoe's confusion is that she thinks there is a perfect correlation between drinking and physical or mental problems in the child, so that if Dick's mother had not drunk he would have been better, even if Zoe can't point to the particular way in which Dick would have been better. But the correlation isn't perfect, it's only a statistical link.

Example 4 Lack of education causes poverty. Widespread poverty causes crime. So lack of education causes crime.

Analysis We often hear words like these, and some politicians base policy on them. But they're too vague. How much education constitutes "lack of education"? How poor do you have to be? How many poor people constitute "widespread poverty"? Researchers make these sentences more precise and analyze them as cause-in-population claims, since we know they couldn't be true general causal claims: There are people with little education who have become rich; and lots of poor people are law-abiding citizens. Indeed, in the worst years of the Depression in the 1930s, when there was more widespread poverty than at any time since in the U.S., there was less crime than any time in the last 20 years. This suggests it would be hard to find a precise version of the second sentence that is a true cause-in-population claim.

5   Explanations, Models, and Theories

We give explanations and encounter others
every day. They are a big part of how we make
sense of our lives. In Section 5.1 we'll see that
many of the tools for evaluating arguments and
cause and effect can be used to analyze
explanations. We'll also see how to avoid
making common mistakes in reasoning with
explanations.

Explanations are closely linked to models
and theories, which are essential in every area of
science and social science. In Section 5.2 we
look at a series of examples of models and
theories to understand better what it means for
an experiment to confirm a model and how one
theory can be better than another.

5.1 Explanations

Why does the sun rise in the east? How does electricity
work? How come Spot gets a bath every week? Why didn't
you give me an A on the last exam?

We give explanations as answers to lots of different
kinds of questions. Our answers can be as varied as the
questions. We can give a story, a myth about how the world
was created. We can write a scientific treatise on how the
muscles of the esophagus work. We can give instructions for
how to play a guitar. We can draw a map.

Here we will focus on verbal explanations, particularly
ones that answer the question "Why is this true?"

> **Explanations** An explanation is a collection of claims
> that can be understood as "E because of A, B, C, . . .".
> We call A, B, C, . . . the *explanation* and E the claim
> being explained. Sometimes the entire inference is
> referred to as the explanation.
>
> An *inferential explanation* is one that is meant to
> answer "Why is E true?"

An inferential explanation is meant to show *why* a claim
is true. That's different from an argument to show *that* the
claim is true. With an explanation we should already have
good reason to believe, say, "The sky is blue," and we want
to show what that claim follows from. The explanation
should provide us with other claims from which it follows.

Example 1 —Why is the sky blue?
—Because sunlight is refracted through the air in such a way
that other wavelengths are diminished.
Analysis This is an inferential explanation. The explanation

is "Sunlight is refracted through the air in such a way that wavelengths other than blue are diminished"; it is meant to explain "The sky is blue."

What conditions are needed for an inferential explanation to be good?

1. The claim that's meant to be explained is very plausible. We can't explain what's dubious.

Example 2 Dick: Why is it that most people who call psychic hotlines are women?

Zoe: Wait a minute, what makes you think more women than men call psychic hotlines?

Analysis Dick has posed a **loaded question**: a request for an explanation of a claim that is not highly plausible. Zoe has responded appropriately, asking for an argument to establish that "More women than men call psychic hotlines" is true.

2. The explanation answers the right question. Questions are often ambiguous, and a good explanation to one reading of a question can often be a bad explanation to another. If a question is ambiguous, then that's a fault of the person asking the question—we can't be expected to guess correctly what's meant. An explanation is bad because it answers the wrong question *if* it's very clear what question is meant.

Example 3 Mother: There were two pieces of cake in the cupboard. Why is there only one now?

Child: Because it was dark and I couldn't see the other piece.

Analysis This is a good explanation—to the wrong question.

3. The claims doing the explaining are plausible. In an inferential explanation the claims doing the explaining are supposed to make clear why the claim we are explaining is true. They can't do that if they are implausible.

Example 4 The sky is blue because there are blue globules in the atmosphere.

Analysis This is a bad explanation because "There are blue globules in the atmosphere" is not plausible.

4. The explanation is valid or strong. In an inferential explanation the truth of the claim being explained is supposed to follow from the claims doing the explaining. So the relation between those claims should be valid or strong, like the relation between the premises and conclusion of a good argument.

Example 5 Dogs lick their owners because they aren't cats.

Analysis This is a bad explanation. The relation of "Dogs aren't cats" to "Dogs lick their owners" is neither valid nor strong, and there's no obvious way to repair it.

As with arguments, *we allow that an explanation might need repair.* An explanation "E because of A" might require further claims to supplement A. But *a good inferential explanation will have at least one claim among those that do the explaining that is less plausible than what's being explained.* Otherwise it wouldn't explain—it would convince. A good explanation is not a good argument.

Example 6 Zoe (to Dick): You drank three cocktails before dinner, a bottle of wine with dinner, then a couple of glasses of brandy. Anyone who drinks that much is going to get a headache.

Analysis Zoe offers a good explanation of why Dick has a headache:

Anyone who drinks that much is going to have a headache.
Therefore (explains why), Dick has a headache.

Judged as an argument this is bad, for it begs the question: It's a lot more obvious to Dick that he has a headache than that anyone who drinks that much is going to have a headache.

5. The explanation is not circular. We can't explain why a claim is true by just restating the claim in other words.

Example 7 Zoe: Why can't you write today, Dick?

Dick: Because I have writer's block.

Analysis This is a bad explanation. "I have writer's block" just means that Dick can't write.

> ### Necessary conditions for an inferential explanation
> ### to be good   For "E because of A, B, C, . . ." to be a
> good inferential explanation the following must hold:
>
> * E is highly plausible.
> * A, B, C, . . . answer the right question.
> * Each of A, B, C, . . . is plausible, but at least one
>   of them is not more plausible than E.
> * "A, B, C, . . . therefore E" is valid or strong, possibly
>   with respect to some plausible unstated claims.
> * The explanation is not "E because of D" where
>   D is E itself or a simple rewriting of E.

Often we say an explanation is *right* or *correct* rather than "good," and *wrong* rather than "bad."

Causal explanations   Sometimes an explanation is given in terms of cause and effect. If it's good causal reasoning and the explanation answers the right question, then the explanation is good; otherwise, it's bad.

Example 8   —Why did Dick wake up?
   —Because Spot was barking.
   Analysis   This is a good causal explanation (recall p. 86).

Explanation 9   Customer: Why did you call your coffee house *The Dog & Duck*?
   Owner: Because *The Duck & Dog* doesn't sound good.
   Analysis   This is a bad explanation. The inference from "*The Duck & Dog* doesn't sound good" to "I called the coffee house *The Dog & Duck*" is weak, and there's no obvious way to repair it.

Explanation 10   Customer: Why did you call your coffee house *The Dog & Duck*?
   Owner: Why not?
   Analysis   This is a bad explanation. Shifting the burden of proof is just as bad for explanations as for arguments.

Example 11 Suzy: Why did Dick just get up and leave the room like that in the middle of what Tom was saying?

Zoe: Because he wanted to.

Analysis This is a bad explanation. We want to know why Dick wanted to leave the room. Wanting to leave the room when Tom is talking is something unusual and requires further explanation. An explanation is *inadequate* if it leads to a further "Why?" Even if the claims doing the explaining are obviously true, they may not be what we normally expect.

Example 12 Zoe: I can see that this argument is bad. But why?

Dr. E: The argument is bad because it's weak, for example, Sheila could have been a rabbit or a herring.

Analysis Assuming that Dr. E knows what he's talking about, this is a good inferential explanation. But an explanation in terms of rules or criteria isn't causal.

Example 13 Lee: Why did Mr. Johns, the owner of that fast-food restaurant where your mom works, lower prices on all the meals?

Suzy: It's because he's got a good heart and wants poor people to be able to enjoy his food.

Zoe: I don't think so. He was the one who opposed soup kitchens in town.

Suzy: He's just covering up. He's afraid of being thought a nice guy. He can't face his unconscious wish to be loved.

Analysis Is Suzy's explanation good? The evidence Zoe has points to the explanation being false. Of course what Suzy says could be true. But there's no way to test whether that's Mr. Johns' motive, since he's either hiding it or it's unconscious.

Untestable claims are the worst candidates for a good explanation. Claims about hidden or unconscious motivation particularly are a dime a dozen and can explain anything; they just can't explain anything well.

The relation of explanations to arguments

Dick, Zoe, and Spot are out for a walk in the countryside. Spot runs off and returns after five minutes. Dick notices that Spot has blood around his muzzle. And they both really notice that Spot stinks like a skunk. Dick turns to Zoe and

says, "Spot must have killed a skunk. Look at the blood on
his muzzle. And he smells like a skunk."

Dick has made a *good argument*:

Spot has blood on his muzzle. Spot smells like a skunk.
Therefore, Spot killed a skunk.

Dick has left out some premises that he knows are as obvious
to Zoe as to him:

Spot isn't bleeding.
Skunks aren't able to fight back very well.
Normally when Spot draws a lot of blood from an
    animal that is smaller than him, he kills it.
Only skunks give off a characteristic odor that drenches
    whoever or whatever is near if they are attacked.
Dogs kill animals by biting them and typically drawing
    blood.

Zoe replies, "Oh, that explains why he's got blood on his
muzzle and smells so bad." That is, she takes the same claims
and views them as an explanation, a *good explanation*,
relative to the same unstated premises:

Spot killed a skunk
explains why Spot has blood on his muzzle and smells
    like a skunk.

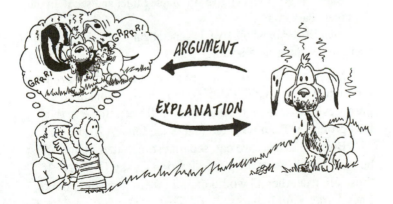

Given an explanation "A *explains* E " (perhaps relative to some other claims), we can ask what evidence we have for A. Sometimes we can supply all the evidence we need just by reversing the inference, using the *associated argument*: "E therefore A" (assuming those other claims as premises). In the example above, for Zoe's explanation to be good, "Spot killed a skunk" must be plausible. And it is, because of the associated argument that Dick gave—we don't need to wait until Dick and Zoe find the dead skunk.

Often, though, we have to supply further claims to establish A.

Example 14   Spot chases cats because he sees cats as something good to eat and because cats are smaller than him.

Analysis   "Cats are smaller than Spot" is plausible, but "Spot sees cats as something good to eat" is not obviously true. The associated argument for it is:

Spot chases cats and cats are smaller than Spot.
Therefore, Spot sees cats as something good to eat.

This is weak. Without more evidence for "Spot sees cats as something good to eat" we shouldn't accept the explanation.

The relation of explanations to predictions

Example 15   Flo: Spot barks. And Wanda's dog Ralph barks. And Dr. E's dogs Anubis and Juney bark. So all dogs bark.

Barb: Yeah. Let's go over to Maple Street and see if all the dogs there bark, too.

Analysis   Flo, who's five, is generalizing. Her friend Barb wants to test the generalization.

Suppose that A, B, C, D are given as inductive evidence for a generalization G. (Some other plausible unstated premises may also be needed, but we'll keep those in the background.) Then we have that G explains A, B, C, D.

But if G is true, we can see that some other claims must be true, instances of the generalization G, say L, M, N. If those are true, then G would explain them, too (Fido barks, Lady barks, Buddy barks, . . .). That is, G *explains* A, B, C,

D and *predicts* L, M, N, where *the difference between the explanation and the prediction is that we don't know if the prediction is true.*

Suppose we find that L, M, N are indeed true. Then the argument "A, B, C, D + L, M, N therefore G" is a better argument for G than we had before. At the very least it has more instances of the generalization as premises.

How can more instances of a generalization prove the generalization better? They can if (1) they are from different kinds of situations, that is A, B, C, D + L, M, N cover a more representative sample of possible instances of G than do just A, B, C, D. And this is typically what happens. We deduce claims from G for situations that we had not previously considered. And (2) because we had not previously considered the kind of instances L, M, N of the generalization G, we have some confidence that we haven't got G by manipulating the data, selecting situations that would establish just this hypothesis.

A good way to test an hypothesis or generalization is to try to falsify it. Trying to falsify a generalization just means we are consciously trying to come up with instances of the generalization to test that are as different as we can imagine from A, B, C, D. Trying to falsify is just a good way to ensure (1) and (2). We say an experiment *confirms*—to some extent—the (doubtful claims in the) explanation if it shows that a prediction is true.

Comparing explanations

Given two explanations of the same claim, which is better? If one is right and the other wrong, the right one is better. If both are acceptable, we prefer the one that answers the right question and that doesn't leave us asking a further "Why?"

We also prefer a *simpler* explanation: its premises are more plausible, it is more clearly strong or valid (unstated premises are obvious and more plausible), and it has fewer steps. All else being equal, we also prefer the stronger one.

Example 16 Zoe: How was your walk?
Dick: Spot ran away again just before we got to the yard.
Zoe: We better get him. Why does he run away just before you come home?
Dick: It's just his age. He'll outgrow it. All dogs do.

Analysis This sounded like a good explanation, until Dick and Zoe found that Spot chased a cat up a telephone pole in the field behind their house.

The explanation of the example is not bad. Perhaps in a year or two when Spot is better trained, he won't run away even to chase a cat. But there is a better explanation: Spot ran away because he likes to chase cats. It's better because it's stronger.

Some scientists think that if they have an explanation that explains a lot and which is the best anyone's offered, then it must be true.

> It can hardly be supposed that a false theory would explain, in so satisfactory a manner as does the theory of natural selection, the several large classes of facts above specified [the geographical distribution of species, the existence of vestigial organs in animals, etc.]. It has recently been objected that this is an unsafe method of arguing; but it is a method used in judging of the common events of life, and has often been used by the greatest natural philosophers.
>
> Charles Darwin, *On the Origin of Species*

But if Darwin was right, why did scientists spend the next hundred years trying to confirm or disprove the hypothesis of natural selection? Only now do we believe that a somewhat revised version of Darwin's hypotheses are true. It's the *fallacy of inference to the best explanation* to say that because some claims constitute the best explanation they are therefore true. That's just arguing backwards: From the premises (explanation) we can argue to true claims, so the premises are true. Besides, we don't have accepted criteria for what counts as the best explanation, and anyway, it's only the best explanation we've thought of so far. Scientists have high hopes for their hypotheses, and are motivated to investigate them if they appear to provide a better explanation than current theories. But the scientific community quickly corrects anyone who thinks that just making an hypothesis establishes it as true.

Example 17 Maria: Why do I have such pain in my back? It doesn't feel like a muscle cramp or a pinched nerve.

Doctor: A kidney stone would explain the pain. Kidney stones give that kind of pain, and it's in the right place for that.

Analysis The doctor's explanation is "Your back hurts because you have a kidney stone." This would have been a good explanation if the doctor and Maria had good reason to believe it. But at that point the only reason they had was the associated argument, which wasn't strong. Still, it was the best explanation at that time.

So the doctor made predictions from the explanation: "A kidney stone would show up on an X-ray," "You would have an elevated white blood cell count," and "You would have blood in your urine." He tested each of these and found them false. If the explanation were true, each would very likely be true. Therefore, (reducing to the absurd) the explanation is very likely false.

Nothing else was found, so by process of elimination the doctor concluded that Maria had a severe sprain or strain, for which exercise and education were the only remedy. The doctor was right to investigate whether the best explanation he had at the time was really true before he did surgery for a kidney stone.

Finding an explanation that is better than all others (that you've happened to consider) does not justify belief in the premises. It only provides motive to investigate whether it's true.

This the best explanation we have.
= This is a good hypothesis to investigate.

Teleological explanations

One day while cleaning out the small pond in his backyard Dr. E asked himself:

Why is there a filter on this wet-dry vacuum?

The wet-dry vacuum had a sponge-like filter, but the vacuum

sucked up water a lot faster without it. He wondered if he could remove the filter.

Dr. E wanted to know the function of the filter. A causal explanation could be given starting with how someone once designed the vacuum with the filter, invoking what that person thought was the function of the filter. But most of that explanation would be beside the point. Dr. E didn't want to know why it is *true* that there's a filter on the vacuum, even though the truth of that claim is assumed in the question. He wanted to know the *function* of the filter. Some explanations should answer not "Why is this true?" but "What does this do?" or "Why would he or she do that?"

> *Teleological explanation*   An explanation is teleological (tee-lee-ah-logical) if it invokes goals or functions, or uses claims that can come true only after the claim being explained is true.

Example 18   —Why is the missile going off in that direction?
   —Because it wants to in order to hit that plane.
   Analysis It's a bad *anthropomorphism* to ascribe goals to a missile: People, not missiles, have goals. We can and should replace this teleological explanation with an inferential one: "The missile has been designed to go in the direction of the nearest source of heat comparable to the heat generated by a jet engine. The plane over there in that direction has a jet engine producing that kind of heat." *Often a teleological explanation is offered when an inferential one should be used.*

In science we prefer not to use teleological explanations. After all, if the explanation uses claims that can be true only after the claim being explained becomes true, then it can't be causal (the cause has to precede the effect), and it would seem that the future is somehow affecting the past.

A request for a teleological explanation assumes that the object has a function, or that the person or thing has a goal or motive. That is part of what's being assumed. But often there is simply no motive, no function, no goal, or at least none we can discern. The right response, as to a loaded question, is to ask why someone should believe there is a function or motive. The *teleological fallacy* is to argue that because something occurs in nature it must have a purpose.

Example 19 Dick (picking his nose): Why do humans get snot in their nose that dries up and has to be picked away? I can't understand what good it does.

Zoe: What makes you think there is a function? Can't some things just be? Maybe it just developed along with everything else.

Analysis Zoe correctly points out Dick's teleological fallacy.

But the biggest problem with teleological explanations is that we don't have criteria for what counts as a good one. That's because we don't have a clear idea how to judge what counts as the function of something. At best, as we've seen, we can say that for a teleological explanation "E because of A, B, C, . . ." to be good: (1) E should be highly plausible, (2) the explanation should answer the right question, (3) it shouldn't be circular, and (4) it shouldn't ascribe motives, beliefs, or goals to something that can't have those.

Example 20 —Why will the Atlanta Braves win the pennant?
—Because they have the best pitching staff.

Analysis This sounds like an explanation, but it isn't: "The Atlanta Braves will win the pennant" is not obviously true. It's a prediction. If the prediction comes true, then it will be further evidence for the general claim "The team with the best pitching staff always (usually?) wins the pennant."

Example 21 —Why did Ponce de Leon wander all over the area we now call "Florida"?
—Because he was looking for the fountain of youth.

Analysis This is a teleological explanation. But it can be replaced with a better inferential explanation: "Ponce de Leon wandered over Florida because he believed there was such a thing as the fountain of youth and that it was there."

Example 22   Tom: Why is this towel under the door?
      Suzy: In order to keep the draft out.
      Analysis   Here is a teleological explanation in terms of the function of the object. But what if there is a draft under the door even with the towel there? We can talk about functions and unfulfilled functions, but it seems easier to answer the question with an inferential explanation: "Because Suzy thought that putting the towel under the door would keep out the draft."

Example 23   —Why do mammals have lungs?
      —So that they can breathe.
      Analysis   This is not a good inferential explanation: "Mammals can breathe, therefore mammals have lungs" is either weak or circular. Yet this seems to be a good explanation if what is wanted is an answer about the function of lungs. In biology nowadays such explanations are usually replaced by ones in terms of evolutionary fitness.

Example 24   Why does the blood circulate through the body?
      (1) Because the heart pumps the blood through the arteries.
      (2) In order to bring oxygen to every part of the body tissue.
      Analysis   The first explanation is a good causal one, if it answers the right question. The second is a good teleological one, if it answers the right question.

5.2 Models and Theories

What is a model? How do we determine if a model is good? How can we modify a model in the light of new evidence?

Example 1   A map of Minersville, Utah—reasoning by analogy

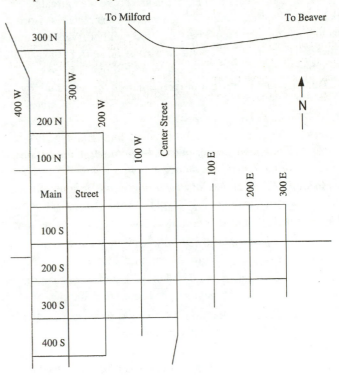

This is an accurate map of Minersville, Utah. Looking at it we can see that the streets are evenly spaced. For example, there is the same distance between 100 N and 200 N as between 100 E and 200 E. The last street to the east is 300 E. There is no paved road going north beyond Main Street on 200 E.

That is, from this map we can deduce claims about Minersville, even if we've never been there. But there is much we can't deduce: Are there hills in Minersville? Are there lots of trees? How wide are the streets? How far apart are the streets? Where are there houses? The map is accurate for what it pays attention to: the relative location of streets. But it tells us nothing about what it ignores.

Reasoning about Minersville from this map is reasoning by analogy. The map is similar to Minersville in the relative position of streets and their orientation to North. The differences between the map and Minersville aren't important when we infer that the north end of 200 W is at 200 N. Perhaps you've seen a scale model of a city or a mountain. Such a model abstracts less from the actual terrain: height and perhaps placement of rivers and trees are there. The map of Minersville *abstracts more* from the actual terrain than a scale model of the city would: *it ignores more.*

This map highlights that *models are used for reasoning by analogy: We can draw conclusions when similarities are noted and the differences don't matter.*

Example 2   The kinetic theory of gases—getting true predictions doesn't mean the model is "true"
"This theory is based on the following postulates, or assumptions.
1. Gases are composed of a large number of particles that behave like hard, spherical objects in a state of constant, random motion.
2. The particles move in a straight line until they collide with another particle or the walls of the container.
3. The particles are much smaller than the distance between the particles. Most of the volume of a gas is therefore empty space.
4. There is no force of attraction between gas particles or between the particles and the walls of the container.
5. Collisions between gas particles or collisions with the walls of the container are perfectly elastic. Energy can be transferred from one particle to another during a collision, but the total kinetic energy of the particles after the collision is the same as it was before the collision.
6. The average kinetic energy of a collection of gas particles depends on the temperature of the gas and nothing else."

J. Spencer, G. Bodner, and L. Rickard, Chemistry

Here is a picture of what is supposed to be going on in a gas in a closed container. The molecules of gas are represented as dots, as if they were hard spherical balls.

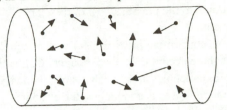

The length of the line emanating from a particle models the particle's speed; the arrow models the direction the particle is moving. The kinetic energy of a particle is defined in terms of its mass and velocity: kinetic energy = .5 mass x velocity^2.

The model defines what is meant for a collision to be elastic. In contrast, here is a picture of what happens in an inelastic collision between a rubber ball and the floor. Each time the ball hits the ground, some of its kinetic energy is lost either through being transferred to the floor or in compressing the ball.

The kinetic theory of gases abstracts very much from what a gas in a container actually is: Molecules of gas are not generally spherical and are certainly not solid; the collisions between molecules and the walls of a container or each other are not perfectly elastic; there is some gravitational attraction between the particles and each other and also with the container. That is, there are a lot of differences between the model and the actual behavior of gases.

But there are enough similarities for the model to be useful. The model suggests that the pressure of a gas results from the collisions between the gas particles and the walls of the container. So if the container is made smaller for the same amount of gas, the pressure should increase; and if the container is made larger, the pressure should be less. So the pressure should be proportional to the inverse of the volume of the gas. That is, the model suggests a claim about the relationship of pressure to volume in a gas. Experiments can be performed, varying the pressure or volume, and they are close to being in accord with that claim.

Other laws are also suggested by the model: Pressure is

proportional to the temperature of the gas, where the temperature is taken to be the average kinetic energy of the gas. The volume of the gas should be proportional to the temperature. The amount of gas should be proportional to the pressure. All of these are confirmed by experiment.

Those experiments confirming predictions from the model do not mean the model is more accurate than we thought. Collisions still aren't really elastic; molecules aren't really hard spherical balls. The kinetic theory of gases is a model useful, as with any analogy, where the differences don't matter.

Example 3   The acceleration of falling objects—an equation can be a model

Galileo argued that falling objects accelerate as they fall: They begin falling slowly and fall faster and faster the farther they fall. He didn't need any mathematics to show that. He just noted that a heavy stone dropped from 6 feet will drive a stake into the ground much farther than if it were dropped from 6 inches.

He also said that the reason a feather falls more slowly than an iron ball when dropped is because of the resistance of air. He argued that at a given location on the earth and in the absence of air resistance, all objects should fall with the same acceleration. He claimed that the distance traveled by a falling object is proportional to the square of the time it travels. Today, from many measurements, the equation is given by:

(‡) $d = 9.80 \text{ meters} / \text{sec}^2 \cdot t^2$ where t is time in seconds

The equation (‡) is an analogy. It says that if we compare a falling object to an imaginary point mass falling to the earth with no air resistance, then the calculation from the equation (which is really a deduction) will hold for the object, too. The differences don't matter. Or rather, they don't matter very much, since air resistance does slow down an object. Indeed, if an object falls far enough, say if you drop a hat from an airplane, it will reach a maximum velocity when the force of the air resistance equals the acceleration. And it matters where on earth you are: An object dropped from a 100 foot building in San Francisco will accelerate more than an object dropped from a 100 foot building in Denver, 5000 feet above sea level. We can only draw conclusions where the differences don't matter.

*Example 4   Newton's laws of motion and Einstein's theory of
relativity— how a false theory can be used*
Newton's laws of motion are taught in every elementary physics
course and are used daily by physicists. Yet modern physics has
replaced Newton's theories with Einstein's and quantum
mechanics. Newton's laws, physicists tell us, are false.

But can't we say that Newton's laws are correct relative to the
quality of measurements involved, even though Newton's laws
can't be derived from quantum mechanics? Or perhaps they can if
a premise is added that we ignore certain small effects. Yet how is
that part of a theory?

Newton's laws of motion are "just like" how moderately large
objects interact at moderately low speeds; we can use those laws to
draw conclusions (make calculations) so long as the differences
don't matter. Some of the assumptions of that theory are used as
conditions to tell us when the theory is meant to be applied.

*Example 5   Ether as the medium of light waves—a prediction
can show an assumption of a theory is false*
In the 19th century light was understood as waves. In analogy with
waves in water or sound waves in the air, a medium was postulated
for the propagation of light waves: the ether. Using that
assumption, many predictions could be made about the path and
speed of light in terms of its wave behavior. Attempts were made
to isolate or verify the existence of an ether. But the predictions
that were made turned out to be false. When a better theory was
postulated by Einstein, one which assumed no ether and gave as
good or better predictions in all cases where the ether assumption
did, the theory of ether was abandoned.

*Example 6   Euclidean plane geometry—a model that can't
be true*
Euclidean plane geometry speaks of points and lines: a point is
location without dimension, a line is extension without breadth.
No such objects exist in our experience. But Euclidean geometry
is remarkably useful in measuring and calculating distances and
positions in our daily lives.

Points are abstractions of very small dots made by a pencil or
other implement. Lines are abstractions of physical lines, either

drawn or sighted. So long as the differences don't matter, that is, so long as the size of the points and the lines are very small relative to what is being measured or plotted, we can deduce conclusions that are true.

No one asks (anymore) whether the axioms of Euclidean geometry are true. Rather, when the differences don't matter, we can calculate and predict using Euclidean geometry. When the differences do matter, as in calculating paths of airplanes circling the globe, Euclidean plane geometry does not apply, and another model, geometry for spherical surfaces, is invoked.

Euclidean geometry is a deductive theory: A conclusion drawn from the axioms is accepted only if the inference is valid. It is a purely mathematical theory, which taken as mathematics would appear to have no application since the objects of which it speaks do not exist. But taken as a model it has applications in the usual sense, arguing by analogy where the differences don't matter.

Models and analogies

We have seen models of static situations (the map) and of processes (acceleration of falling objects). We have seen examples of models that are entirely visual and of models formulated entirely in terms of mathematical equations. We have seen models in which the assumptions of the model are entirely implicit (the map), and we have seen models in which the assumptions are quite explicit (Newton's laws of motion). Above all, we have seen that drawing conclusions from a model is reasoning by analogy.

We do not ask whether the assumptions of the model are true, but whether we can use the model in a given situation: Do the similarities that are being invoked hold, and do the differences not matter? Even in the case of Newton's laws of motion, where it would seem that what is at stake is whether the assumptions are true, we continue to use the model when we know that the assumptions are false in those cases where, as in any analogy, the differences don't matter. In only one example (the ether) did it seem that what was at issue was whether a particular assumption of the theory was actually true of the world.

The assumptions of theories in science are false when we consider them as representing *all* aspects of some particular part of our experience. The key claim in every analogy is false in the same way. When we say that one side of an analogy is "just like" the other, that's false. What is true is that they are "like" one another in some key respects which allow us to deduce claims for the one from deducing claims for the other.

The term *model* is typically applied to what can be visualized or made concrete, while the term *theory* seems to be used for examples that are fairly formal with explicitly stated assumptions. But in many cases it is as appropriate to call an example a theory as to call it a model, and there seems to be no definite distinction between those terms.

Confirming a theory

From theories we can make predictions. When a prediction turns out to be true, we say it **confirms** (to some degree) the theory. But this is not the same as confirming an explanation, for it rarely makes sense to say the claims that make up a theory—the assumptions of the theory—are true or false.

We cannot say that verifications of the relation of pressure, temperature, and volume in a gas confirm that molecules are hard little balls and that all collisions are completely elastic. We cannot say that fitting a carpenter's square exactly into a wooden triangle that is 50cm x 40cm x 30cm confirms the theorem of Pythagoras. Nor can we say that finding a tree at the corner of 100 W and 100 S in Minersville disconfirms the model given by the map. The map wasn't meant to give any information about trees, so it doesn't matter that it shows no tree there.

Except in rare instances where we think (usually temporarily) that we have hit upon a truth of the universe to use as an assumption in a theory, we do not think that the assumptions of a theory are true or false. We can only say of a theory such as Euclidean plane geometry or the kinetic theory of gases whether it is *applicable* in a particular situation we are investigating.

To say that a theory is applicable is to say that, though there are differences between the world and what the assumptions of the theory state, those differences don't matter for the conclusions we wish to draw. Often we can decide if a theory is applicable only by attempting to apply it. We use the theory to draw conclusions in particular instances, claiming that the differences don't matter. If the conclusions —the predictions—turn out to be true (enough), then we have some confidence that we are right. If a prediction turns out false, then the model is not applicable there. We do not say that Euclidean plane geometry is false because it cannot be used to calculate the path of an airplane on the globe; we say that Euclidean plane geometry is inapplicable for calculating on globes.

When we make predictions and they are true, we confirm a range of application of a model. When we make predictions and they are false, we disconfirm a range of application, that is, we find limits for the range of application of a model. More information about where the model can be applied and where it cannot be applied may lead, often with great effort, to our describing more precisely the range of application of a model. In that case, the claims describing the range of application can be added to the theory. We often use mathematics as a language for making this art of analogy precise. But in many cases it is difficult to state precisely the range of application. Reasoning using models is reasoning by analogy, after all, which is likely to require judgment.

Sometimes it's said that a theory is valid, or is true, or that a theory holds, or that a theory works for . . . . These are just different ways to assert that a particular situation or class of situations to which we wish to apply a theory is within the range of that theory.

Good theories and how to modify theories in the light
of new evidence

We've seen that the criteria for whether a theory is good or
better than another cannot in general include whether the
assumptions of the theory are true or "realistic."

Besides getting true predictions, what other criteria can
we use to evaluate a theory? Consider what we do when we
discover that a prediction made from a theory is false.

When Newton's laws of motion result in inaccurate
predictions for very small objects, we note that the theory had
been assumed true for all sizes of objects and then restrict the
range of application. But when the theory of the ether
resulted in false predictions, no modification was made to the
theory, for none could be made. That theory did not abstract
from experience, ignoring some aspects of situations under
consideration, but postulated something in addition to our
experience, something we were able to show did not exist.
The theory was completely abandoned.

If a theory has been made by abstraction, that is, many
aspects of our experience are ignored and only a few are
considered significant, then tracing back along that *path of*
abstraction we can try to distinguish what difference there is
between our model and our experience that matters. What
have we ignored that cannot in this situation be ignored?
If we cannot state generally what the difference is that
matters, then at best the false prediction sets some limit on
the range of applicability of the model or theory. We cannot
use the theory here—where "here" means this situation or
ones that we can see are very similar.

But our goal will be to state precisely the difference that
matters and try to factor it into our theory. That is, we try to
devise a complication of our theory in which that aspect
of our experience is taken into account. As with Einstein's
improvement of Newton's laws, we get a better theory that is
more widely applicable and which explains why the old
theory worked as well as it did and why it failed in the ways

6 Writing and Making Decisions

6.1 Writing Good Arguments

With what you've learned here, you should be better able to evaluate claims and arguments that you encounter every day. And with some practice, you should be able to construct good arguments. Writing down a good argument, though, seems to require more practice, unlearning many of the tricks of padding out essays. Though there isn't space in this text to give you that practice, you'll have lots of opportunities in your courses and your work. Here we summarize some points that will be helpful.

- If you don't have an argument, literary style won't salvage your essay.

- If the issue is vague, use definitions or rewrite the issue in order to present a precise claim to deliberate.

- Don't make a clear issue vague by appealing to some common but meaningless phrase, such as "This is a free country."

- Beware of questions used as claims. The reader might not answer them the way you do.

- Your premises must be highly plausible, and there must be glue, something that connects the premises to the conclusion. Your argument must be impervious to the questions: "So?", "Why?"

- Don't claim more than you actually prove.

- There is often a trade-off: You can make your argument strong, but perhaps only at the expense of a rather dubious premise. Or you can make all your premises clearly true, but leave out the dubious premise that is needed to make the argument strong. Given the choice, opt for making the argument strong. If it's weak, no one should accept the conclusion. And if it's weak because of an unstated premise, it's better to have that premise stated explicitly so it can be the object of debate.

- Your reader should be able to follow how your argument is put together. Indicator words are essential.

- Your argument won't get any better by weaseling with "I believe that" or "I feel that." Your reader probably won't care about your feelings, and they won't establish the truth of your conclusion.

- Your argument should be able to withstand the obvious counterarguments. It's wise to consider them in your essay.

- For some issues, the best argument may be one which concludes that we should suspend judgment.

- Slanters turn off those you might want to convince; fallacies just convince the careful reader that you're dumb or devious.

- If you can't spell, if you can't write complete sentences, if you leave words out, then you can't convince anyone. All the reader's effort will be spent trying to decipher what you intended to say.

You should be able to distinguish a good argument from a bad one. Use the critical abilities you've developed to read your own work. Learn to stand outside your work and judge it, as you would judge an argument made by someone else.

If you reason calmly and well you will earn the respect of the other person, and may learn that others merit your respect, too.

6.2 Making Decisions

The skills you've learned here can help you make better decisions.

Making a decision is making a choice. You have options. Make a list for and against the choice—all the pros and cons you can think of. Make the best argument for each side. Then your decision should be easy: Choose the option for which there is the best argument. Making decisions is no more than being very careful in constructing arguments for your choices.

But there may be more than two choices. Your first step should be to list all the options and give an argument that these really are the only options, and not a false dilemma.

Suppose you do all that, and you still feel there's something wrong. You see that the best argument is for the option you feel isn't right. You have a gut reaction that it's the wrong decision. Then you're missing something. Don't be irrational. You know when confronted with an argument that appears good yet whose conclusion seems false, you must show that the argument is weak or a premise is implausible. Go back to your pro and con lists.

Now that your reasoning has been sharpened, you can understand more, you can avoid being duped. And, we hope, you will reason well with those you love and work with and need to convince. And you can make better decisions. But whether you will do so depends not just on method, not just on the tools of reasoning, but on your goals, your ends. And that depends on virtue.

Index

abstraction, path of, 123
accepting/rejecting a claim,
  criteria for, 22
advertising, 23
affirming the consequent, 48
"all", 52
"almost all", 56
alternatives, 42
analogy, 64
  legal reasoning and, 68
  models and, 120–121
  refuting an argument by,
    67–68
  steps in evaluating, 67
anecdotal evidence, 81
antecedent of a conditional, 45
anthropomorphism, 112
appeal to authority, 23
appeal to common belief, 24
appeal to emotion, 35
appeal to fear, 36
appeal to pity, 36
apples and oranges, 69
applicability of a model, 122
arguing backwards, 23
  and inference to the best
    explanation , 110
arguing backwards with "all", 54
arguing backwards with "no", 55
argument, 12
  associated, 108
  good —, tests for, 17
  steps to check for
    validity/strength, 16
  strong/weak, 14

argument (continued)
  unrepairable, 30.
    See also fallacy.
  valid, 14
associated argument, 108
authority,
  accepting a claim because of,
    20–23
  appeal to, 23
average, 70

begging the question, 14
biased sample, 78
burden of proof, 9

causal claim, 86
causal explanation, 105
causal factor, 95
cause and effect, 86
  a cause, 95
  causal factor, 95
  common cause, 89–90
  general, 86
  intervening cause, 96
  necessary criteria for, 90
  normal conditions for, 88
  particular, 86
  reversing, 91
  tracing too far back, 90
cause in population, 97
claim, 2
coincidence, 91
composition, fallacy of, 67
compound claim, 42
conclusion, 12
conditional claim, 45
  contradictory of a, 45–46
confidence level, 83

Richard L. Epstein received his B.A. *summa cum laude* at the University of Pennsylvania and his Ph.D. in Mathematics at the University of California, Berkeley. He held a postdoctoral fellowship in mathematics and philosophy at Victoria University of Wellington, New Zealand, before an extensive career teaching mathematics and philosophy. He has been a Fulbright Scholar to Brazil and a National Academy of Sciences Scholar to Poland. He also owned and managed the Dog & Duck Coffee House. He is the author of the series of research texts *The Semantic Foundations of Logic* as well as *Critical Thinking* and *Five Ways of Saying "Therefore"*. Currently he is head of the Advanced Reasoning Forum in Socorro, New Mexico.

Carolyn Kernberger received her B.G.S. *cum laude* from New Mexico Tech and her M.A. in Teaching English as a Second Language at the University of New Mexico. She has taught in the United States, Japan, and at the College of Micronesia FSM, where she was also the Accreditation Officer.

Together they have also written *The Guide to Critical Thinking in Economics*.

Advanced Reasoning Forum
Imagine the Possibilities

www.AdvancedReasoningForum.org